DEFYING

JIHAD

The dramatic true story of a woman who volunteered to kill infidels— and then faced death for becoming one

DEFYING ☪ JIHAD

ESTHER AHMAD
with CRAIG BORLASE

TYNDALE
MOMENTUM®

The nonfiction imprint of Tyndale House Publishers, Inc.

Visit Tyndale online at www.tyndale.com.

Visit Tyndale Momentum online at www.tyndalemomentum.com.

TYNDALE, Tyndale Momentum, and Tyndale's quill logo are registered trademarks of Tyndale House Publishers, Inc. The Tyndale Momentum logo is a trademark of Tyndale House Publishers, Inc. Tyndale Momentum is the nonfiction imprint of Tyndale House Publishers, Inc., Carol Stream, Illinois.

Defying Jihad: The Dramatic True Story of a Woman Who Volunteered to Kill Infidels— and Then Faced Death for Becoming One

Designed by Dean H. Renninger

Published in association with the literary agency of D.C. Jacobson & Associates LLC, an Author Management Company. www.dcjacobson.com.

All Scripture quotations, unless otherwise indicated, are taken from the Holy Bible, *New International Version,*® *NIV.*® Copyright © 1973, 1978, 1984, 2011 by Biblica, Inc.® Used by permission. All rights reserved worldwide.

Scripture quotations marked NLT are taken from the *Holy Bible*, New Living Translation, copyright © 1996, 2004, 2015 by Tyndale House Foundation. Used by permission of Tyndale House Publishers, Inc., Carol Stream, Illinois 60188. All rights reserved.

For information about special discounts for bulk purchases, please contact Tyndale House Publishers at csresponse@tyndale.com, or call 1-800-323-9400.

Library of Congress Cataloging-in-Publication Data
Names: Ahmad, Esther, author.
Title: Defying Jihad : the dramatic true story of a woman who volunteered to kill infidels— and then faced death for becoming one / Esther Ahmad with Craig Borlase.
Description: Carol Stream, Illinois : Tyndale House Publishers, Inc., 2019. | Includes bibliographical references.
Identifiers: LCCN 2018036560| ISBN 9781496425881 (hc) | ISBN 9781496425898 (sc)
Subjects: LCSH: Ahmad, Esther. | Christian converts from Islam—Pakistan—Biography.
Classification: LCC BV2626.4.A36 A3 2019 | DDC 248.2/4670092 [B] —dc23 LC
record available at https://lccn.loc.gov/2018036560

Printed in the United States of America

25   24   23   22   21   20   19
7   6   5   4   3   2   1

This book is dedicated to my husband, John, and my daughter,
Amiyah. You have risked so much by being with me, and there
is not a day that passes when I don't thank God for you.
I pray that God will continue to bless and protect you.

Contents

Author's Note ix
Prologue xi

Part 1
Everyone Has to Die Sometime *1*

Part 2
You Will Be Hated by Everyone *65*

Part 3
Do Not Worry about What You Will Say *161*

Part 4
Go to Another Land That God Will Give You *223*

Q and A with Esther Ahmad 289
Notes 295
Discussion Questions 297
About the Authors 303

Author's Note

This memoir is the true story of my journey from growing up in a militant Muslim family to my life-changing encounter with Jesus. For the protection of my family—both those who remain in Pakistan and those in the United States—I have changed some of the names and specific locations, and in the case of my children, I have created a composite character to safeguard their identities.

I would also like to acknowledge that my story is just that—my story. Not all Muslims are extremists, and not all Muslims interpret jihad the way my community did. I hope this book gives you a window into a life you may not know much about, and I hope it encourages dialogue among people of various cultural and religious backgrounds.

Prologue

I step back from the window and try to ignore the noise of the mob gathering outside my home. They are even more agitated than the last time they came and shattered the nighttime peace of our quiet, respectable street. They *should* be agitated. After what I have done and who I have become, it is only a matter of time before their anger turns to rage.

Standing in the entryway, I close my eyes, but I can still see them bathed in the orange glow of a single streetlight. The young men with their mouths twisted in anger, fists punching in the air. The women, their faces hidden behind burkas, leaning from the windows of neighboring houses. The old men watching from the side, their eyes fixed on the man in the middle of them all. The man with more power than any of them.

My father.

I exhale and work harder to still my thoughts. I let the individual cries of "Allahu Akbar!" and "Bring out the girl!" blur and fold into one another. I don't want to hear their voices, and I don't want to see their faces. Not because I am scared, though. I am—a little. But fear is the last thing I need right now.

I just need to be able to think. I want to cast out my anchor and steel my mind against these fierce currents that are pushing past me, trying to drag me down into panic. I want to hold on to what is real. Whatever is coming next, I must hold fast to my faith.

I bring to mind the book I was given, one of the two books I have kept secret from almost everyone else in my house. Behind its creased and faded cover are tales of men and women who died professing their allegiance to God. The deaths described are brutal, but the power of their stories is enough to make my breath quicken within my chest and my heart swell with hope.

I have read those stories again and again—so many times that I know them as well as I know the fig trees and guava trees in the courtyard. Right now, they are the only living things separating me from the mob.

I think about the other book I have hidden—the one with the black leather cover and the pages so thin I am always afraid I will tear them if I do not handle them with the greatest of care. I think about the stories those pages contain. I think about Paul and Stephen and so many others who died a martyr's death.

Did they feel this same fear I feel when they faced their mob? Did their minds race and their hearts rage as the end drew near? Did they struggle the way I do now, battling to keep their thoughts on the eternity after death instead of the moments before it? If they did, is there hope for me?

My life is paper thin right now. My time here on earth is about to end. I am ready to arrive in heaven. But leaving earth behind? That is harder. Will I be erased from my family's story? Will they forget about me? Will the memory of me be wiped out?

The noise from outside takes a leap forward, like a tiger pouncing on its prey. Someone has opened the front door. I squeeze my eyes, willing them to remain shut. I can feel the warm summer breeze on my cheek.

I hear my mother's voice mingling with the crowd. Is she shouting at someone? I have to ignore her, too.

Daniel. That is who I choose to think about. I picture him facing the mob calling for his death; I see him being thrown into the den of lions, trusting that God and God alone is in control. I recall Daniel's three friends, too, as strong hands pushed them closer to the furnace. I do not even have to imagine the heat—I can practically feel it on my own arms.

I remember the fourth man who was seen among the flames—the man nobody could name but everybody could see. The man who turned the mob and the whole kingdom back to God. The man who changed everything.

I open my eyes to see my mother standing in front of me, her face framed with a veil. She arranges a *dupatta* on my head, covering my hair and the lower part of my face with the cloth. She is staring into my eyes with tears in her own.

"Send her out!" says a deep voice behind her. My father's voice is always the loudest.

I can tell my mother wants to say something, but the words catch in her throat. We embrace, and I feel her tears on my cheeks.

"Remember that he is our refuge," I tell her. "He is our deliverer and our ever-present help in trouble. Whether I live or die, Jesus Christ will come to rescue me. To rescue us both."

I follow my father out the door and through the courtyard. I keep my head down, counting the steps that take me past the fig trees and guava trees and into the street.

Only when my father stops do I look up and take it all in.

He turns around to face me, but I know he will not look at me. Instead, his eyes survey the crowd. I let mine follow his.

The mob is bigger than I thought it would be. There must be two or three hundred people here. Their anger is fiercer than I expected too, and I can feel their hatred, sense it burrowing into me.

"Shoot her!" one of the young men near me shouts.

I glance at him briefly. His beard is wispy, barely covering his chin. I wonder if I have ever met him before.

Soon others join in, adding in cries of *"Kafir!"*—branding me an infidel. But the noise around me means nothing to me. Something far more powerful is happening within.

It happens in an instant. Suddenly I am filled with an otherworldly kind of courage. I feel the words churn within me like a chemical reaction. Like phosphorus burning in a lab, they burst into life and force their way out.

"Yes!" I shout. "Kill me!" My voice is loud, louder than I ever remember it being. And it is strong, too. As new as this voice is, I know it is mine. This is me speaking, from the deepest part of me.

"If you want to shoot me, then do it," I spit, looking straight at the boy with the half beard. "But do not do it here. Take me to the main junction and let the whole city know. I want everyone in Pakistan to hear that today I am giving my life to Jesus Christ."

There is the briefest moment of silence before a man behind me shouts, "Cut her!"

"Yes!" I spin around to see him holding a blade as long as his hand. The words are coming faster and louder now, the furnace within me growing hotter and hotter. Even if I wanted to, I could not stop myself from speaking like this. Nothing could silence me right now. "You can cut my throat, but I believe God is powerful and mighty to do incredible things—yesterday, today, and forever! If you kill me, I believe that many people will hear about what happened to me and ask who Jesus is. And when they seek him, they will find him!"

"Burn her!"

"Yes!" I say. "Burn me, and I believe I will go with him and he will come down. You will all see his glorious face, and many of you who are standing here will see that he is the true God. However you kill me, many of you will become Christians this very day!"

Everything slows down as I look around me. In that moment, I see more clearly than I ever have in my life. I can see the blindness in the men shouting their hatred at me. I sense the fear and the pain in the women with their veils, hiding behind walls and windows. I know that not too long ago, I was like them. I was wounded and lost, a lone sheep that had strayed too far and had lost all hope of reaching safety.

But not now. Now I am ready. My struggle is over. I am ready to die. I close my eyes and exhale a silent prayer of thanks. Soon it will be over. Soon I will be . . .

"Wait." My father's voice cuts through the noise of the crowd. My prayer turns to stone, and my blood becomes lead.

I open my eyes. He is standing close to me—so close that I can smell the faintest hint of his cologne. If I wanted to, I could reach out and touch him.

I cannot remember the last time we were this close.

I cannot remember ever being this close.

He is looking behind me, but I am staring at him, studying his face the way I used to study samples under a microscope. From this close, the familiar seems strange and foreign. From this close, nothing about my father is the way I remembered. He looks old. Weary.

"Wait," he says again. For the first time I can remember in all my twenty-one years, his eyes lock onto mine.

The look he gives me is not the look of a father. It is not a look of love or kindness or care. It is not the way my mother looks at me. My father stares at me through the eyes of a man who feels nothing for what he sees.

"I have a better idea," he says. He blinks twice and turns away.

I do not know what he is planning, but I know what he is thinking. He sees me differently now. He sees me as his jihad. Somehow, I will have to pay.

Part 1

EVERYONE
HAS TO DIE
SOMETIME

1

I was wounded the moment I came into this world. Not that
there was a problem with my birth—I was born strong and
healthy, with a cry loud enough to shake the trees. Nor was
there anything wrong with my mother. She cried with delight
when she saw me, took me to her breast, and looked with
love on my full head of dark hair and my wide-eyed stare. She
welcomed me just as she had welcomed her first two babies
when they were born one year and two years earlier.

The wound came from my father.

He wanted a son. I was his third daughter.

The first time my mother gave birth to a girl, he had
accepted it as the will of Allah. He was a little more reluctant
the second time it happened. But to be given three daughters?
It was not good. Why had he not yet been blessed with a son?
How could a man hold up his head with pride when his wife
had given him nothing but daughters?

And so, instead of coming to visit me and give me a name after my birth as he had done for my sisters, he refused to see me. He didn't tend to my mother or look at me with pride. He didn't visit the mosque to pray or invite the *ulema* to visit us at home as every good father should. Unlike my sisters and the other children born in our neighborhood, I had no visit from a scholar, nobody to whisper the call to prayer into my newborn ears, informing me that there is no god but Allah, that Muhammad is the messenger of God.

Instead, my father buried himself in his work. From sunrise to sunset, he traveled the city, buying and selling spices just as his father before him had done. When he came home at night, he made a point of avoiding the room where my mother was crying, surrounded by relatives and friends who tried, and failed, to console her. He ignored my mother's tears and the gentle advice from people who told him not to be angry and to accept that a third daughter was clearly Allah's will.

After three days, he finally gave in. He entered the bedroom where my mother was quietly nursing me. "Business has been good," he said, explaining his change of heart. "Perhaps Allah has chosen to bless me after all."

He inquired after my mother's and my health, then turned to leave.

"We will call her Zakhira," he said as he walked out the door.

†

Even though I grew up being known by a name that means "wealth," I felt like a beggar. The story of my first three days followed me around everywhere I went. It was the first thing people would mention when I met them. I lost count of the times I was introduced by my mother at a gathering with extended family and heard, "Oh, so *this* is the girl your husband refused to look at, eh?"

The sound of their clicking tongues as they feasted on the gossip twisted the knife within me. It was one thing to be unloved by my father, but the fact that everyone else knew it made the wound even deeper.

The older I got, the more questions I asked of Allah. At prayers, kneeling alongside my sisters, who taunted me for being the one my father never wanted, I would press my head onto the musty-smelling mat and pray silently while tears filled my eyes. *Why hadn't my father accepted me? Why had Allah made me a girl? Why punish me from my first breath?*

I never heard any answers.

Instead, I started to name the feelings that stirred within me. Emptiness. Loneliness. Restlessness. Was there nothing I could do to get my father to see me?

†

My mother became pregnant again, delivering into my father's open arms the son he had always wanted. Another girl came along too, and there were times when it seemed like things were finally changing for me. Like the season when my father would bring one child at a time with him on a trip to the market. He was rigorously fair, and whenever it was my turn, he allowed me to select the chicken we'd eat that night or the spices my mother required at home.

"I know you will choose well, Zakhira," he would say to me. "You're lucky. You brought me a lot of money."

Precious as those memories are, what I remember most are the other conversations that occurred in the market. When we bumped into one of his old friends, they would stare at me and ask, "Who is this? Is it the third one? The one you wouldn't look at?"

My father never said he was sorry, and I never spoke to him or my mother about it. It was not the kind of conversation a girl in Pakistan could have with her parents. The only choice I had was to deal with the pain myself.

Prayer helped. I learned to pull the sheet over my head at night and call out to Allah, whispering in my own language, Urdu, as the tears escaped my eyes.

When I was seven, I enrolled at school, as my older sisters had done before me. That's when I stumbled across a brand-new way of dealing with my troubles: I discovered I could make my father proud.

After several weeks of lessons, my parents were called in to a special meeting with my teacher. I sat beside my father and mother, my eyes fixed on my feet as my legs swung from the edge of the chair.

I listened as the teacher spoke at length about what a good student I was. "She's very well behaved, always respectful, and very organized. She's the smartest in her class and loves to ensure that the other girls are sitting down and not disturbing me."

I looked up to see my mother staring at me. Through the slit in her veil, I could see her eyes dancing, and I knew that beneath the black fabric was a smile as wide as an ocean. But it was my father's reaction that most took me by surprise.

"Yes." He looked straight at the teacher, his hands spread wide as if he were about to accept a gift. "We are very proud of her."

His voice was somber, but the words were like honey to me. I could feel them make their way deep inside me, soothing and healing as they went.

I wasn't surprised that he didn't look at me once during that meeting or that he never mentioned the teacher's words to anyone else. I wasn't surprised that my sisters renewed their teasing of me with even greater vigor later that day. But I vowed to do better, to work even harder. Maybe once I did, my father would finally look at me.

†

Perhaps because my father was cold and distant, my relationship with my mother was especially close. She and I talked constantly, and when school finished for the day, I took delight in walking alongside her as she picked her way through the chaos and color of the local market. Together we would duck into a low building, past the thin curtains that hung in the doorway. Those curtains marked the end of the outside world and the beginning of my mother's kingdom. It was there, in the low-ceilinged room lit by the lights that buzzed gently overhead, that my mother ran her dressmaking business.

It was a magical place. I would sit on the stool beside her and look around, my eyes wide as my mother and her team of two other women sat surrounded by piles of brightly colored cloth. There were endless rivers of silks and cottons, boxes of buttons, and the constant chatter of three electric sewing machines. They were old and dented, but they could still perform miracles. They turned lifeless material into dresses that were every bit as beautiful as those I saw in magazines.

I was desperate to find out everything I could about those machines. I peppered my mother with questions about how they worked. I was a little disappointed the day my mother showed me the foot pedal that started and stopped the motor. Until that point, I'd honestly believed the machines had a life of their own. I soon got over the disappointment, however, and started begging my mother to allow me to try one of the machines myself.

"When you're older," she said. She guided me to a dress that was finished apart from the buttons. "First you must learn how to sew as I did."

No men ever came in through the curtain. My older sisters visited only occasionally, and I don't remember my brother ever coming. Sometimes I had to share my mother's attention with my younger sister, but I didn't mind much. There was enough magic for both of us in that little room.

All the women would remove their burkas as soon as they were inside. They could talk freely in the workshop, and there were days when the air was full of laughter. Other times everyone was quiet, but whatever the mood, I always felt safe within those walls.

When I wasn't asking how electricity worked or quizzing my mother about how the needle combined the two threads together so neatly, the conversation often turned to matters of religion. Not that I did so much asking. My mother steered those conversations, teaching me what it meant to be a good Muslim with even more passion than she taught me how to sew on a button.

"You must always give praise to Muhammad and give thanks to Allah," she would say almost daily. "Remain pure, Zakhira. Don't let yourself be taken off the path the Prophet has marked out for us."

She had a beautiful singing voice, but the only kind of songs she sang were *naats*—songs that praise Muhammad. She never allowed us to go to the movies, even though my older sisters begged her to let them see the latest Indian blockbuster their friends were talking about. And even though she ran a successful business making beautiful dresses, she was careful to do so without straying from Islam.

"If you wear nail polish, Allah will pluck out your nails,"

she would say. "Wear lipstick, and your lips will get sewed up with metal. Can you imagine how painful that would be?"

I could if I tried hard enough, but my mind was too full of thoughts about electricity and the engineering of the sewing equipment to worry too much about makeup, romantic Bollywood movies, or eternal damnation.

†

When I finished my second year of school, I gladly spent the days of summer break with my mother in the workshop. That was the summer when I took my first steps as a seamstress, watching in awe as the sewing machine growled into life when I pressed the pedal.

It was also the summer I learned about hell.

The conversation happened on an afternoon like any other. When my mother and I were sitting alone in the workshop, she shifted the topic away from makeup and movies. As she spoke, a darkness fell across my mind.

"If someone lies," she said, "Allah will pull their tongue out hard and nail it against the wall."

The image was so vivid and shocking that it took me a while to respond. When I could finally speak again, my voice sounded far away. "How does Allah know when we lie?"

"There are two angels watching over you all the time—one on your left shoulder and one on your right. The one on the left writes down every bad thing you do, while the one on the right keeps a record of everything you do that's good."

I thought about my father and all the times I'd felt angry with him. I felt a chill run down my back. When I spoke next, my voice was even weaker.

"Ami, what if I have thought bad thoughts about someone? Does the angel on the left write those down too?"

My mother smiled and reached out to stroke my cheek. "No, my child. They can't hear your thoughts. It's only our actions that count." She paused, and the smile faded from her face. "Everybody dies someday, and when they do, they will find themselves standing in front of Allah. On one side will be the angel who has written down the good, and on the other will be the angel who has written down the bad. In front of Allah will be a set of weighing scales. If the good deeds outweigh the bad, the person goes to heaven. If the bad are heavier, they go to hell."

Later that evening, my mother and I were at home, preparing the evening meal with my sisters. As I was baking *chapattis*, my concentration wavered and I burned my arm on the pan. The pain was immediate, though I did my best to swallow my tears.

Throughout the rest of the evening, I checked the welt on my arm. I was convinced that I could feel my flesh continue to burn. Even when I went to bed, I was agitated and anxious, my arm still too sore for me to sleep.

When sleep finally came, my dreams were terrifying. I was standing before a throne made of black stone. On each side stood an angel. As I looked, the angel on the right turned away from me while the angel on the left reached out his hand. I could feel his fingers clasp tightly around the spot on my arm where the pan had burned me. Then I could feel my feet moving as he dragged me beneath the floor.

The closer we got to hell, the hotter it became. Soon my whole body was burning up in the heat, as if every inch of my flesh had been seared by the frying pan.

I awoke in the darkness. My arm was throbbing, and my back was covered in sweat. I tried to call out for my mother, but for the longest time no sound came.

2

I was not the only one my mother sought to educate about the importance of being a good Muslim. She encouraged my siblings to pray and emphasized to all of us the realities of the judgment we would face after death. But while I was an attentive, thoughtful listener, the same could not be said for everyone in my family. Especially my father.

The first battle of their marriage was over his closet. My father favored Western dress, but to my mother, his polyester pants and skintight shirts were an outward sign of a lack of inward devotion to Allah. He was a weaker man then compared to his later years, and he gave in soon enough, accepting the plain, flowing *shalwar kameez* that his new bride suggested. It was a hollow victory, however, for in the years that followed, my father showed no sign of becoming a more devoted servant of Allah. He dressed the part, but his heart was not in it.

One night I woke to the sound of shouting outside. I joined

my giggling sisters at the window and watched as my father, dressed in the tightest-fitting pants I had ever seen and a white shirt with a collar almost as wide as his shoulders, banged on the door.

"Let me in!" he shouted.

"No." My mother's voice drifted up from inside the house. "I don't want you coming in here if you're going to dress like that and go to the cinema."

There was a pause. "Okay," my father said, his voice calm and gentle. "I won't go again. So let me in."

"No!" my mother shouted, full of the confidence that came from knowing she was acting as a dutiful daughter of Allah. "Let everyone see you've been locked out."

The battle was over, but the war raged on. Several months later, my father walked into the house carrying a brand-new television. We had never owned one before, and like all my siblings, I was thrilled. It was hard for my mother to get us out to school the next morning, and we all rushed home at the end of the day, excited to see what wonders were in store for us on the screen.

To our surprise, there was a gap where my father had placed the TV.

"I sold it," my mother said as we stood there, openmouthed. "I don't want a TV in my home. If it stayed, Allah's blessed angel wouldn't come to us." I didn't like it, but I couldn't argue with her logic. My mother had told me so many times about the importance of not defiling ourselves. To serve Allah dutifully, we must follow all the steps laid out in the Qur'an—how to pray, how to eat, how to dress, and even how to greet each other. According to the hadith, angels do not enter a house where there are animate pictures, so why would a good Muslim family even contemplate bringing a TV into their home?

When my father came home and discovered what had happened, he did what he'd done all along in his marriage. He said nothing and walked out.

†

My mother set all the rules for the house. She made sure all her children prayed at home five times a day, and she saw to it that the Qur'an was always the highest book in the room and was never placed on the floor. In order to encourage the blessed angel to visit our home, she ensured that no unclean animal such as a dog ever came through the doors.

Our family wasn't unusual in this regard. Our street was full of families just like ours, in which the mothers took care of their children and homes and the fathers devoted themselves to their businesses. However, even at a young age, I could tell there were times when people treated us differently. Whenever we went to the market to buy rice, lentils, or garlic, the vendors always paid my mother a little more attention than they paid to the other customers. And if my father sent any of us children to the butcher to collect some meat, we would be given the best cuts as well as a cold soda—something none of the other children in the shop received. Wealth brought with it many privileges.

The fact that people respected my father and held him in high esteem didn't mean much to me. All that mattered from my perspective was that I was a disappointment to him. As hard as I worked in school, the moments when I made him proud were few and far between. The taunts from my sisters continued, as did the murmurs and sour faces from the women who gossiped about me whenever I was in their presence. I was still the child my father never wanted. I was still the girl he wished would have been born a boy.

✝

Our whole world changed the day my father grew a beard. At least, that was how it seemed to me at the time.

I was ten years old, and Pakistan was changing. A small group of militant Islamic extremists started recruiting in our area. They wanted to wrest control of Pakistan away from the businessmen and secular leaders who held power. They believed that Pakistan should be ruled by sharia law, and they encouraged our community to reject all the trappings of Western life that so many in our country had embraced. They tried to close down the cinemas and starve the fashion shops of business. In retrospect, I see that they targeted my father specifically because he was wealthy. They had ambitious plans for the future, and one day they would need people to fund them.

I don't know how, but they were able to succeed where my mother had failed. They managed to turn my father's head away from the world of tight-fitting pants and Indian movies and convince him to take his faith seriously.

And so he grew his beard.

The more time he spent with the militants, the longer and fuller his beard became. At first it was patchy, but by the time it was long enough to cover his chin, he had started taking my brother to the mosque at the end of our street to pray five times a day.

By the time his beard was long enough for him to stroke, its strands curling around his fingers, he had announced that our entire family should declare our allegiance to the group.

When the beard was almost as full as the beards of the clerics he talked to on the street, my father remodeled the first floor of the house. He wanted to create a room big enough to invite one hundred people to come and listen to the clerics as they taught about what it means to be a true, devoted Muslim.

Within weeks, the building work was complete. One of the bedrooms was gone, and so was the best room in the house—the place where we had once received guests, seating them in leather armchairs that squatted like thrones along the wall. In their place was a room with wall-to-wall carpeting, a single chair at one end, and a curtain that could be drawn across one corner so that women could attend the meetings at the same time as the men without being seen.

Though this room contained no machines, little color, and nothing in the way of womanly chatter and laughter, I thought it was every bit as magical as my mother's workshop. And after the first meeting I attended there, I was convinced it was a place where miracles could happen.

Once the builders and decorators left, I helped clean the room. My mother led the work, directing all of us children in our tasks and encouraging us with statements like this: "The harder you work, the happier Allah will be."

By the time Friday afternoon came around, I could barely contain myself. I watched from upstairs as a crowd of men gathered outside our gates before being welcomed in by my father. I listened to the house fill with the sound of deep male voices and then quickly took my place alongside my sisters and mother, hidden from view by the curtain.

Since this was the first *daras*, or meeting, my father decided we should mark the occasion by asking Allah to bless the food my mother had prepared: white rice with almonds and cashews mixed in and milk poured over the top. My father's job was to bring in the dish, cover it with a white cloth, and place it near the seat of the cleric, who was to give us instructions on how to pray.

We all closed our eyes, held our prayer beads, and repeated the same Arabic prayer twenty-one times—once for each of the beads. We turned our heads left and right as we prayed. Soon we fell into a rhythm, and the room hummed and stirred just like my mother's workshop when all three sewing machines were running.

"Allahu Akbar!" The loud cry from the front of the room startled me at first. I looked up to see the cleric standing in front of the dish, the white cloth held high.

"The handprint!" another man said. "We have been blessed by the Prophet, peace be upon him."

The room erupted with praise and excitement, and I pushed toward the front so I could see beyond the curtain and witness with my own eyes what everyone was looking at. In the middle of the rice was a clear handprint. It could only have been made by a man, and I saw no reason to doubt that Muhammad himself had made it.

"You see," my mother said as I caught her eye, "the harder we work, the happier Allah will be."

†

After that first daras, we held meetings at our home at least once a week. I never needed to be persuaded to attend. Even if I was the youngest female sitting behind the curtain, I would listen, enthralled, as the clerics taught from the Qur'an (the sacred text revealed to Muhammad by Allah) and the hadith (the additional writings that give further insight into the life and teachings of Muhammad). I learned to love both, to feast on the words as if they were bread.

In those days, I heard a lot about generosity and the importance of helping those in need. Though we were wealthy, I knew I only had to walk a couple of blocks to see poverty on the streets. The more I heard and the more I observed, the more I understood that Muslims are passionate, generous people. When they give, they do so joyfully and without reservation.

Perhaps the best example of such generosity came to me from an unlikely source: my father. I arrived home from school one day to see five sewing machines lined up in the hall and my mother staring at them, confused.

"What are these for?" my mother asked my father when he came home.

"I bought them for the widows," he said.

"Why? You could just have given them the money instead, and they would be able to buy food and send their children to school."

"Perhaps, but this way they will be able to earn money for themselves. And when they do, they, too, will be able to give just as we're doing."

Not long after the sewing machines had been given to their grateful new owners, we hosted a daras I'll never forget. The room was even more crowded than usual, and instead of a single cleric up front, there were five. The men held themselves with a degree of authority and composure I'd never seen before. To my young eyes, these men with their flowing beards and scholarly airs looked like the wisest people I'd ever seen.

The oldest among them spoke for a while about the life of Muhammad and then indicated that the other clerics should each take hold of a corner of a large white sheet. They held up the sheet between them, and at once everyone got to their feet and pressed forward. Most people threw money onto the sheet, but one woman removed a gold bracelet and placed it among the coins and notes.

I ran out of the room and headed upstairs to my bedroom, retrieving the box at the bottom of my closet. In less than a minute, I was back at the daras, my hands letting go of the gold chains and earrings that I'd owned for as long as I could remember. They were the most precious possessions I had, and I wanted to give them to Allah.

Once the meeting was over, I sat quietly on the carpet while the guests drifted out. It felt good to be generous. I wanted to help the poor, but I also wanted Allah to smile on me. I wanted our family to be blessed, and I knew that my gold was a small price to pay for Allah's favor.

A pair of shoeless feet stopped in front of me. I looked up to see my father staring down at me. I felt flustered, nervous to be so close to him.

"Stand up," he said. "Follow me."

When we got out to the front courtyard, my mother was talking to my sisters. My father had me stand beside him and addressed my mother, along with whoever else was within earshot.

"I am proud of this girl!" he said. "She gave the very best she had to give. She did it all for Allah's cause." I was so happy I thought I would burst. "I'm proud of you," he said. "You never thought about yourself."

He looked at my mother again. "Go and buy her some more jewelry. But this time buy bigger, thicker chains."

My sisters looked at me in shock. I allowed myself the briefest of smiles, dropped my eyes to the ground, and gave silent praise to Allah. The thought of being given more valuable jewelry was wonderful, but even that excitement paled in comparison to the joy I felt after hearing my father speak about me like that in public. It was almost too much to take in.

3

I knew it was a risk, but I was desperate. So I pulled my dupatta tighter and walked toward my father and the mullah. The daras had ended a while earlier, but Anwar, the mullah, had remained in the meeting room to talk.

I fell to my knees at the mullah's feet and tried to deliver the brief speech I'd prepared. But instead of "Please, if Allah wills it, may you grant me the privilege of continuing my education?" all that came out of my mouth were wordless sobs.

"Why is she crying?" the mullah asked my father.

I could hear the anger in my father's voice when he spoke. "She wants to go to school next year, but there is no need. She has already completed five years, and what girl needs more than that? She's only going to wash clothes and dishes and work at home. I'll never send her for a job, nor will her husband when she marries. Five years was enough education for her older sisters, and it is enough for her."

I had heard all his arguments already—more than once. Most of the time when my father spoke like this, I felt enraged at him. But as I listened to him in the meeting room that Friday afternoon, I felt overwhelmed with sadness.

The five years I'd spent in school had made a deep impact on me. Education had given me an opportunity to try to win not just my father's approval but also the affirmation of my teachers and fellow students. I had carried out my responsibilities diligently, and I liked being thought of as a leader. I knew that these opportunities were precious, that not every girl in Pakistan could afford even just a few years of education.

Still, there was more to it than glowing report cards and good grades. I liked learning. The school was state run and followed a broad curriculum. The lessons in science and math offered a window into a world that thrilled me—a world where I was allowed, even encouraged, to ask questions. And with every answer came another mystery to try to solve. Studying both satisfied my appetite and left me ravenous for more knowledge. When I was at school, I was no longer the girl my father rejected. I was the pupil outperforming all the others.

Yet I was facing the same predicament that many other girls my age faced. The end of middle school was a natural cutoff point for parents with traditional views like my father. Five years was considered enough education to allow a girl to become the kind of wife they envisioned: submissive, unambitious, and tethered to the home.

I had begged my father to read the words of my final report, to take the advice of the teachers: "We believe Zakhira can go forward. She cannot stop here." But so far my pleading had achieved nothing. And as I pressed my face down at the feet of the mullah, I realized what a fool I was. What was I thinking? Of all the people in the city, this devout follower of Islam was the least likely to grant a twelve-year-old girl's wish for an education.

"How is she in her studies?" he asked.

"Oh, she is very good," my father replied, the anger in his voice replaced by pride. "She has won many trophies for her schoolwork, and her report cards are always exemplary."

"Well," the mullah said after a pause, "if she is good, then perhaps you should let her go. But only to the right school. A child like this needs careful nurturing."

I was stunned and a little confused.

"The madrassa?" my father asked.

"Yes. Of course, she would have to dress appropriately."

"I will!" I shouted. I hadn't worn a burka before, but if that was what it took to stay in school, I was more than willing. "Thank you," I said to the mullah. "You are just like an angel."

✝

At the end of summer break, I enrolled in my new school. Though it was run by clerics from the same militant organization my father was affiliated with, I didn't notice many differences from my old school at first. We still studied math and science, as well as English. We spent more time learning about the Qur'an, but I didn't mind. In fact, those lessons gave me more opportunities to shine.

A few weeks into the first term, I heard about a competition between five different madrassas in the city. The aim was to see which student could give the best presentation about the life of Muhammad. I knew immediately that I wanted to participate—and I wanted to win. My mother had taught me well, and our conversations about the Prophet flowed as easily as the fabric through her sewing machines.

The teachers left the students to prepare on their own, giving us one simple piece of advice: if we told any facts or stories about Muhammad that weren't true, we'd still get a point as long as it sounded good.

I studied hard, questioning my mother about the parts of the Qur'an that I struggled to understand. On the day of the competition, I was so nervous I felt sure I was going to lose the chapattis I had eaten for lunch. I was one of the last to speak, and it was nerve racking to hear the impressive presentations given by the girls and boys before me. Yet while a lot of them told a range of stories, including some I had never heard before, many of my fellow contestants kept their eyes nervously on their papers. Watching them and waiting for my turn, I decided to take a risk.

I stood on the stage and lowered the microphone. My legs were shaking and my stomach felt like it was going to drop out from beneath me, but I folded my paper and placed it on the lectern. I looked out at the hundred people gathered, spotted my mother and a few other relatives, took a deep breath, and began. "Prophet Muhammad, peace be upon him, was born on a Monday morning, sometime in AD 570. It was reported that the mother of Prophet Muhammad, peace be upon him, said that when he was born, a great light shone out of her insides and lit the palaces of Syria."

I paused and looked around. There were nods of approval. I took another breath, glad that I had started well but still terrified that I would make a mistake. "The character of Prophet Muhammad, peace be upon him, can be described as honest, kind, and true in all his words. Three times the angel Gabriel came and hugged him. Prophet Muhammad, peace be upon him, spread Islam and went through trials but did not deny Almighty Allah."

There was more nodding. My heart was finally slowing down from its frantic pace. I said a little more about Islam, making sure that every word was based on the Qur'an and the hadith. I was too scared to make up any stories.

Finally, I was almost done. I ended with a poem about the five pillars of Islam that I had memorized. As the first words formed on my lips, I could feel my lungs grow strong within me. My voice filled the room as I called out, "Allah is One and like no one / He has no partner, nor a son / He is kind and just and wise / And has no form, shape or size."

I sat down to the largest applause of the day. A little while later, I collected my winner's trophy and listened as my teachers and my mother talked about what a good job I had done. I listened as long as I thought necessary to be polite and then asked if I could be excused.

I ran the mile home clutching my trophy, desperate to put it on the shelf in the family room next to my other tokens of success. I rearranged my report cards and the other trophies, placing this latest one in the middle.

I did not hear the footsteps behind me. My first indication that my father was watching was when I heard him say, "That's good, Daughter."

I finished arranging the shelf before turning around to thank him. He had already left the room.

†

I'd never been on a field trip before, so when the teachers loaded all the girls onto one bus and the boys onto another, I was about as excited as I'd ever been. The two male teachers at the front of the bus knew how to work a crowd, and they spent half an hour leading us in a series of chants and shouts, seeing which side of the bus could call out the loudest. As we edged out of the city and into the countryside, it was turning out to be the best day I could remember.

Our destination was an art exhibition that was on display in an old farmhouse. I had never seen anything like this collection of pictures before—mostly flowers and landscapes—but they did not inspire me. I would have preferred a science museum or a visit to a factory. Still, the teachers served up a good picnic, and the ride back was just as much fun as the journey there.

A month later, we boarded the buses for another field trip. Once again, our lungs were bursting and our throats were raw from chanting by the time we reached our destination—a low-slung building on the edge of a dusty village.

The teachers had not told us anything about what we were going to see. I was excited and curious, especially when they led us inside a room full of low wooden benches, dimmed the lights, and turned on a data projector.

I had never seen a piece of equipment like this before. I stared at the rectangle of white light that filled the wall facing us, entranced by the way the light forged across the room and turned the dust into stars.

A mullah appeared at the front of the room. "Today we're going to show you what's happening to our Muslim brothers and sisters around the world."

The white rectangle changed in an instant. In front of us was a boy lying facedown on the ground. At first I thought he was sleeping, though why anyone would choose to sleep on the sidewalk in the middle of a muddy puddle was beyond me. But as I looked closer, I saw that his legs were bent at an impossible angle. His eyes were not shut in peace but swollen over. It was not mud on his face; it was blood.

"This is what our brothers and sisters are facing," said the mullah. "And who is doing this? It's the Christians and Jews."

The images I saw that day were seared into my mind. Women with arms burned by cigarettes. Men with wounds flowing with blood, their faces locked in terror. Bodies stripped naked and beaten so badly that their skin looked like filthy rags. Prisoners who had been shaved and starved and trapped behind wire, their bones protruding so much I wondered how they could even stand.

For each photo that covered the wall, the mullah had a new story to tell. He spoke of Bosnia and Chechnya, of massacres in cities I had never heard of. He explained in explicit terms what was happening in the world: that Muslims living in the West were the victims of cruel persecution.

This was all new to me. I was vaguely aware that Pakistan and India often fought, and I'd heard of the occasional attack on mosques, but to see evidence that we Muslims were actually at war was shocking. It was difficult for me to believe that my brothers and sisters around the world were being attacked and tortured.

But there was no hiding from the truth. My eyes had been opened. For the first time in my life, I knew I had an enemy.

When we had seen the last of the images and the wall was bright white again, the mullah continued speaking. "All of us must feel the pain of this suffering. If you don't, then you are no longer a Muslim. But it's not enough to feel it and do nothing. We must share their pain so we can take revenge. This is our struggle. This is our fight. And one day, it will be your fight too."

As we drove back to the city, silence clung to the bus like a thick fog. I sat staring at the frayed fabric of the seat in front of me. I knew the mullah was right. I could feel my blood boiling—I could almost taste the rage within me.

I did not say anything to my mother when I first arrived

at home. Partly it was because I wanted to be quiet for a while to understand what I had seen and heard. Also, she had been complaining of feeling unwell for some time, and I remember not wanting to scare her with my questions. But after a few days I could not keep the thoughts to myself. I went to find her while she was working in the garden, tending the vegetables she grew.

"Did you know that we're at war, Ami?"

"Who told you that?" she said.

I thought about explaining what I had seen on the field trip, but something inside me told me not to. "There are Christians killing Muslims in the West. Did you know that?"

"Yes." She kept plucking tomatoes from their vines. "But you don't have to be scared. It happens far away from here, and there are hardly any Christians in Pakistan. You're safe from them here."

It had not occurred to me that I might be in danger in Pakistan. I went to bed that night even more troubled than I had been before.

†

We had another field trip the following month, and another the month after. Each time the venue was different, though we always had a wall with images shown on it. Some months those photos were even more brutal than the last. Other times the mullah introduced us to stories of people who had been born Christians but converted to Islam. Apparently there were many hundreds of thousands just like them.

"Islam is growing," the mullah said. "Soon the whole world will bow down to Allah!"

On days like those, the bus rides home were a carnival of joy. Whenever the teachers started up a new chorus of call-

and-response, we would shout louder than ever. Knowing that we were on the winning side—that the whole world would one day worship as we did—was so powerful that it left me feeling a little giddy.

Nothing, however, could compare with the last field trip of the year.

For the first time, there was no projector set up. There were no benches, either, and no sign of the usual mullah. We were ushered to a large, dimly lit room. In the middle was a long table draped with a heavy burlap blanket. We stood in silence, forty pairs of eyes staring at the table, wondering what secrets it was hiding.

I felt no fear. If these field trips had taught me anything, it was that I could trust the mullah and the rest of the teachers at the madrassa. After all, it was thanks to them that I now understood the truth about how the countries in the West were targeting Muslims.

After a few minutes, a door on the other side of the room opened and the mullah stepped in. Behind him was a man I had never seen before. He was about the same age as my father. Across one shoulder he carried a rifle.

The mullah walked over to the table. "Today we're going to show you the tools we use to spread Islam." He pulled hard on the sheet and threw it to the floor beside him.

Though none of us had spoken a word since we entered, the room fell into an even deeper silence. I could feel myself being drawn closer to the table, almost overcome with the desperate urge to reach out and touch what lay upon it. Before my eyes were a half-dozen pistols, three rifles, and at least ten grenades.

I had never seen rifles up close before, even though they were a regular part of life in the city. They seemed more powerful and dangerous now that I was at eye level with them. The same was true for the pistols, and I wondered about the strange writing across them. But it was the grenades that caught my attention the most. Knowing that such power and destruction could be held back by a simple pin was truly mesmerizing. I wanted nothing more than to be able to pick one up and examine it.

Others must have felt the same way, because the mullah stepped in front of us and let out a laugh. "Not today, but one day you will get to handle these."

He spent a few minutes talking about the different weapons. It was only when he pulled the blanket over the table again that I looked around me. Each of my fellow classmates was just as fascinated as I had been.

"The time will come when you'll be ready for all of this," the mullah said as he escorted us out of the room.

Soon we were eating our sandwiches and bananas. I could hear groups chattering about which weapon they liked the best and how they would fight against the infidels as soon as they were old enough. I sat apart. I had no interest in their foolish chatter. I had too many thoughts going on inside my head, and I needed to concentrate.

Why, when the mullah had spoken, did I feel like I was more alive than I had ever felt in my life? Why was my heart beating so quickly? Somehow I knew this moment was significant. But how? What on earth could it mean for my future?

4

After a year of learning at the feet of the mullahs, going on monthly field trips, and hearing that Muslims in the West were the victims of mass persecution at the hands of Christians and Jews, I was suddenly removed from the madrassa.

My mother heard that there was space available in one of the state-run schools in the city. She had nothing against the madrassa, but she hadn't forgotten the praise my first teachers had heaped upon me. She hoped that I might continue my studies and perhaps even be able to attend university one day. Not that we spoke about this much. Dreams like these are so fragile that it is wise not to handle them too often. Better to keep them secret, stashed away from prying ears and eyes.

My father was spending an increasing amount of time with the militants, and to my surprise, he did not protest my mother's decision to pull me out of the madrassa and send me to a more academically rigorous school. Perhaps he was too busy to pay much notice, or perhaps he really didn't care what happened to me. Either way, I felt excited about what the future might hold.

Excited, and nervous, too. My year at the madrassa had taught me a lot about world events but little about science. I was terrified that I would not succeed and my father would put an end to my education, so I committed to studying harder than ever.

The one condition my father placed on my leaving the madrassa was that I would continue to have regular religious training with someone from the mosque. I was assigned to one of the female clerics. Like most of her kind, she spent much of her time educating and leading women and young girls. She was well read and passionate about how to be a devoted Muslim, and I looked forward to these weekly meetings. Spending an hour each week talking about stories in the Qur'an made for a pleasant break from cramming all that science and math.

The further I got into my first term at the state school, the clearer it became that my science and math needed work. My mother discussed the matter with my father, who discussed it with one of the clerics, and soon I had an extra weekly study session on my calendar.

My tutor was Anwar, the same mullah who had persuaded my father to let me attend the madrassa in the first place. He was highly educated, and according to the rumors, he had even studied abroad when he was younger. My mother took me to Anwar's house every Tuesday afternoon. She would wait in the courtyard out front while I went inside for my lesson. I was grateful for his help; while the teachers at the madrassa had struggled to explain things to me, Anwar had a way of making things clear in my mind.

I knew exactly why my father agreed to my study sessions

with Anwar. It was not just that he was educated or wealthy, though his house, with its marble floor and imposing wooden furniture, was on a scale far grander than our own. My father chose him because Anwar was the leader of the militants in the city.

Yet Anwar did not look down upon me for my lack of understanding or my gender or because he held more status and wealth than my family. In fact, he treated me in a way that no other male had treated me. He treated me as an equal. Better than that, he would call me "Daughter." Even though I knew it was a common term of endearment, whenever he said the word, I felt alive inside.

One Tuesday afternoon, as I sat working on a math problem Anwar had given me, I became aware that some men had entered the room. I had been concentrating deeply on my work, but when I heard Anwar tell his visitors that they could talk freely in front of me, explaining who my father was, I started to pay attention. I was careful to keep my eyes fixed on the page in my book.

"The brothers in the mountains need more arms," one of the men said.

"What about the last gold we collected?" Anwar asked.

"We sold it all and bought as many weapons as we could, but it wasn't enough. We still need more."

"How much money do you need?"

The first man mentioned a figure so large I struggled to comprehend it.

Anwar paused. When he spoke again, he sounded almost disinterested. "Very well. Leave it to me, and I'll organize some more collections."

Did this mean that the gold that had been collected at the meetings at our home may have been used to buy weapons?

It was a shocking conclusion, but I could find no other explanation. I was even more stunned by the figures mentioned. Millions of rupees. Tens of thousands of dollars. This was possibly the most impressive thing my young ears had ever heard. Intuitively I knew that this was information I would need to keep to myself.

†

"Do you love English, Daughter?"

I looked up from my books and studied Anwar, thrown completely off balance by the question. My father often raged about how English was the language of infidels. I knew exactly how *he* would expect me to answer the question. But I also knew that Anwar and my father were different.

"Yes," I said, my voice suddenly shaky.

Anwar smiled at me. "That's okay. I have lived in America and the UK, and there's much to learn there. But that learning is only possible if you can read and speak English."

I decided to risk a question. "Why did you go there?"

"University," he said. "I studied engineering in London and then in California."

I was on a roll, so I kept going. "Was it dangerous?"

He shrugged, his smile fading. "What I will tell you is this: there's no country like Pakistan. It's the only place where true followers of Allah can live as we do."

A silence settled on the room for a while. I could feel a hundred questions taking flight within me, but my mouth could not seem to form the words.

It was Anwar who spoke next. "Maybe one day you will go to the West and study or work there. And when you do, you can join the work our Muslim brothers and sisters are already doing in those countries."

"How?"

"If you can speak English and you know how to say the right things, it isn't hard to turn Christians away from their religion and bring them into Islam. Besides, there are many Western boys who would be ready to fall in love with a pretty girl like you."

I could feel my cheeks burning as I turned back to my book.

"I'm serious," Anwar said. "There are many Muslim sisters who go and study in the West, find husbands, and bring them into Islam."

I felt awkward and a little embarrassed, but I knew he was right. On one of the field trips, the mullah had shown several pictures of Pakistani brides standing next to Western husbands. He told us that women have the power to change a husband, especially when they have children together.

To redirect the conversation, I brought up a question that had been percolating in me since one of my Qur'an study sessions with the female cleric. She had shown me the passage about Joseph, but the story seemed incomplete. I had asked her what happened next, but all she would say was that it was in another book. If anyone could tell me more, I was sure it was Anwar.

"You want to read about Joseph?" he asked.

"Yes, and Abraham, too."

"There's only one book that tells those stories. I don't have it here. It's a black-colored book—"

"Can I read it? Where can I get it?"

He stood up. "It is called the Bible. It's a Christian book, and you can only get it from them, but you shouldn't have anything to do with those people. Maybe one day I'll find one for you. But for now, you just need to read the Qur'an."

5

I had a clear reason for wanting to do well at school. More than gaining my father's approval—which had become an increasingly remote possibility the more deeply involved he became with the militant group—I had a single, clear goal in mind. I wanted to be a doctor. Specifically, I wanted to be a cardiologist. I did not want to fix just any stranger's heart; I wanted to help my mother. If I didn't, I knew she would die.

My mother's health had started to deteriorate when I was at the madrassa. Sometime after I changed schools, she had been diagnosed with a heart condition, and lately the pain had been increasing. The doctors knew exactly what was wrong and that she would continue to get worse. They even had a plan for surgery that would restore her to full health again. But there was one problem: the only surgeons capable of carrying out the operation in our local hospital were men. For both my mother and my father, this was a deal breaker.

No matter how much I begged her to change her mind and allow them to operate, she refused.

"If I die in surgery after a man has touched me, I will die unclean. I would rather live in pain and die a good Muslim than risk facing Allah like that and be sent to hell."

It was a conversation we repeated often, and it always had the same ending. My mother would look at me and say, "Everyone has to die sometime."

As her body weakened and her pain increased, my own frustrations mounted. I grew to understand my mother's desire to avoid Allah's judgment, and I even came to see her commitment with a degree of respect. What bothered me was that the older I got, the more unlikely it seemed that I would be able to help. Even with Anwar's tutoring and an upturn in my grades, every hospital visit reminded me that there was little room for female doctors in my community. Now that I was sixteen, I could see that I was pushing an impossibly large boulder up a mountain. How could I ever hope to succeed?

At the same time that I began to doubt my own abilities, I started to ask questions of the world around me.

It happened at the hospital one morning. I was sitting next to my mother while she was having tests done. As she lay there wired to a couple of machines, I peeked around the back of one of them. It read, "Made in Germany."

I checked the other machine. "Made in the UK."

In the days that followed, I was on a mission to determine the source of all the medical equipment that was helping my mother. Sure enough, it all came from the West. That prompted me to wonder about other inventions, so I looked in reference books in the school library. I researched everything from the telephone, tape recorders, and monitoring machines to bullets, bombs, and cell phones. I could not find a single invention that came from a Muslim nation. And almost every inventor's name was Christian or Jewish.

All along, the same question rang loud and clear in my head: *Why?*

Why would Allah give so much wisdom to the infidels instead of to us, his beloved and faithful followers?

And why, when I'd been told all my life that people in the West were not good, did they seem so happy all the time? Every advertisement and newspaper photograph I saw showed them smiling. Why, if they were living so badly and in need of being saved, did Allah not make them sad? It did not make sense.

And if Muslims really were the beloved of Allah, why would he allow our enemies to beat and burn and kill us? Why didn't Allah send an angel to destroy them?

It was as if I'd picked a thread at the end of an old rug. The more closely I looked at things, the more everything seemed to unravel, and the more questions I had.

Inevitably, I did what my mother and Anwar had taught me and turned to the hadith. I remembered a famous story I had read about Muhammad's followers who were hiding in a valley called She'eb Abi Talib. People were chasing them, and since they had no food, they had no choice but to eat the grass. Their suffering lasted for three years. When I compared this story to the account in the Qur'an about Moses hitting the rock and water gushing out or Allah providing the Jews with bread as they wandered in the wilderness, it made no sense. Why would Allah feed the infidels but let his own people starve?

These thoughts would force their way into my mind without warning, but it was when night had fallen and the house was still that I heard them the loudest. There in my room, where all was silent apart from the sound of my older sister's deep breathing, I would feel the anger rise within me. I would rage against Allah, shouting silently at him for treating his people so poorly and for treating our enemies so well.

My fury never lasted more than a few seconds. Almost as soon as I released the anger, I felt the fear rise within me. My chest would pound, and my stomach would twist. Raging at Allah was not something a good Muslim was supposed to do. At times like those, I would climb out of bed, walk to the prayer room, and kneel on the floor, begging for Allah's forgiveness, desperately hoping that he wouldn't block his ears to my cries.

✝

My rebellion, such as it was, was not confined to matters of theology and science. Like teenage girls on every continent, I entered a phase when I fought with my mother regularly about fashion. All those afternoons spent in her workshop had nurtured in me a deep love of dresses and style, and the older I got, the more opinionated I became about what I liked.

Of all my mother's magazines at the workshop, my favorite was the one full of photos of rich people getting married. I spent hours staring at the women in their white dresses, tiaras sparkling on their heads. I even managed to smuggle a couple of issues of the magazine home, where I could continue my browsing uninterrupted.

"When I get married," I announced to my mother one day after we had returned from the market, "I want to wear a white dress."

She made a noise that was midway between a snort and a cough.

"What?" I said. "Why not?"

"Red is the best color to marry in. White is what you wear when you are mourning the loss of a husband."

"But why should the color of a dress make any difference to anyone?"

"Zakhira, it just does. Everybody knows that to wear white when you aren't mourning is to invite death. It's the same with black. A woman wears black only when she wants to curse someone. If she wears it at any other time, her brother will die. Now stop this nonsense, and put the garlic away."

I was halfway up the stairs when she finished talking. When I returned to the kitchen a few minutes later, she screamed.

"What are you doing, Zakhira?"

I stood in the doorway, smiling. I did not particularly like the heavy black dress I had changed into—the cut was all wrong, and it was a little too big on me. But this was not about fashion. This was about logic—and making a statement to my mother.

"I just want to see if my brother dies or not."

"What?" she yelled. "You want to kill your brother?"

"No," I said calmly. "I just want to see whether what you say is true or not."

It took hours for my mother to calm down and agree that my brother was still alive and well. After several days of my arguments, she finally agreed to let me wear black again if I wanted to. Still, it wasn't much of a victory for me. What I really wanted was to be able to wear white, like the brides in the magazines. And I longed to make sense of my religion, to know that it could withstand a little testing.

Shortly after this act of defiance, I made a dress for myself that was like the ones I admired in the bridal magazines. I found some white cotton in my mother's workshop and spent weeks embroidering a delicate pattern by hand all around the neck. All the other women there admired it, and even my mother commended me on the quality of my work. But she still refused to let me wear it.

When a family wedding approached, I began lobbying harder than ever. For days on end, I tried to convince my mother to allow me to wear the dress. "Everyone says it's beautiful," I begged over and over. "Why won't you let me wear it? What are you afraid of?"

It was no use. She would always dismiss me with a wave of her hand and a roll of her eyes. In response, I would turn and storm out of the room.

I'd return and try again after a few hours, but my mother was immovable.

And so on the day of the wedding, being every bit as stubborn as she was, I stayed home alone while everybody else in the family went.

Did I regret it? No. A part of me knew that it was foolish to fight over something as insignificant as a dress. Deep down, I knew that it was not about the dress itself. I had found a crack in my religion, a fault line that bothered me. If my own mother, who had taught me so well what it means to be a good Muslim, could be bound by such a foolish and illogical superstition, what else had she gotten wrong?

†

It was Anwar who helped me to see things more clearly and put a halt to my questioning.

"I have a question that has been troubling me," I said one day when I was about to leave his house. "Why did Almighty Allah choose to feed Moses and the Jews but not Muhammad, peace be upon him, and his followers?"

"You shouldn't think so deeply, Daughter," he said with a

smile. "Don't think deeply about Allah, and don't read deeply into the Qur'an. Don't think about each and every word; otherwise you'll go astray. You'll end up questioning Allah himself."

I could feel the blood rush into my head as he spoke. Did he know about my angry outbursts toward Allah?

"I'm sorry," I said, regretting that I had asked the question. "I won't think about these things anymore."

I was desperate for the conversation to be over, but I could feel Anwar's eyes on me. The silence weighed heavily, and I could feel my heart beat faster.

When he spoke again, his voice was quiet but firm, as if he were giving instructions to a child. "Do you know what happens when you die?"

I searched Anwar's face, wondering what he was trying to tell me. I said that I knew a little—that my mother had explained to me about the angel on the left and the angel on the right and how all our good deeds will be weighed against the bad.

"That's all true," he said. "And how you live here on earth will determine how you are rewarded in heaven. For those who serve Allah the most, paradise will be the best. Women will sleep on beds as soft as roses, surrounded by pearl-white cushions. Each one will have a garden surrounded by a high wall that no man can peer over. Anything you want will be just a thought away. If you wish, you can even keep your earthly husband. And the men who are rewarded the most will each receive seventy-two virgins, whose very sweat will be fragrant like perfume."

My mother had told me most of this already, but I still shifted awkwardly in my seat as he spoke.

"Those who never listened to Allah or who never accepted

Muhammad, peace be upon him, as the last prophet will stay in hell forever. They will be thirsty because of the great heat, but the only drink available to them will be boiling water that burns all the way down or pus so vile it could make the strongest stomach sick."

Anwar waited awhile, letting the image swirl in my mind. "That is the choice you face: spend your life as a dedicated follower of Allah and receive the rewards, or choose to turn from him and endure an eternity of punishment. Everyone has to die."

†

My mother had her own plan to make sure I stayed true to following Allah. She told me that I needed to pray more.

"This life is temporary, Zakhira-jan," she said, using an Urdu term of endearment. I stood beside her in the kitchen as we peeled the garlic and washed the lentils. "We need to prepare ourselves for the next life. When you die, the first question the angel will ask is—"

"Are you a Muslim?" I knew the script well enough already.

"That's correct. And what will the angel ask next?"

"Did you offer your prayers?"

"Yes. And then you'll have to recite them. Hell will last longer for those whose voices are mute, and heaven will come sooner for those who know all five of the daily prayers. If you don't know them when you're alive, how are you going to remember them when you're dead?"

We repeated some version of this conversation every week, and eventually the message sank in. Between my mother's counsel and Anwar's advice, my questions faded and my anger was snuffed out. I put the white dress in the back of my closet and devoted myself to being a good Muslim.

I pursued my religious obligations with the same fervor I had used in my science classes. In addition to praying the usual five times a day, I decided to offer three more daily prayers. I started at 3:30 a.m., knowing that these early-morning prayers brought with them extra rewards.

When my mother's health allowed, she joined me, but more often I was alone. I didn't mind at all. It felt good to know that everybody else was sleeping while I was bowing to Allah in prayer, earning my eternal reward. When I was in school and the clock approached 10:00 a.m., I would excuse myself and walk alone to the prayer room. No one else was ever there. In a school of more than two thousand students, I was the only one who was this dedicated.

At home my father would often take my brother to the mosque to pray, leaving us females at home. I would stand in front of my sisters and lead the prayers. Nobody complained or questioned my right to do so. I wasn't the oldest, but I was the most devoted of my siblings, and it seemed only right that I would lead.

Even though I had given up questioning Allah about things like science and the infidels, I still tried to view my religion from a logical perspective. One day I would have to face judgment for my life, and I figured that if five daily prayers were good, surely eight daily prayers were better. I convinced myself that all these extra prayers were a way of tipping the scales in my favor.

But there was one question that haunted me day and night: Were my prayers enough? As hard as I tried, I couldn't be sure I could do enough to secure my place in heaven.

The question burrowed deep inside, echoing endlessly within my mind. This unease set me on edge, leaking into me like oil in a lake. I did my best to ignore it, trying to pray more diligently and recite the Qur'an more regularly.

Some days, though, this struggle to secure my own salvation seemed beyond me. And I didn't know where to turn for help.

6

The first time I heard about jihad, something within me soared. *Yes,* I thought. *This is the way I must live.*

I was at home attending a daras when the mullah shared a simple story.

"After Uthman embraced Islam, he married the Prophet's second daughter and later became the third caliph of Islam. This cost him dearly. His relatives were enraged, and they tortured him, leaving Uthman no choice but to leave behind his wealth and flee the land. Years passed, and Uthman regained his former prosperity. But instead of hoarding his riches in the anticipation of future troubles, he gave generously. More than once, he spent a great portion of his resources on the welfare of Muslims, and when some poor refugees approached him and asked for help, he gave away most of the wheat from his stores, although merchants were willing to pay great sums for the grain. When asked why he had done this, Uthman replied,

'I will get a greater reward from Allah.' In time he came to be known as Al Ghani, which means 'generous.' We are all called to take up the jihad against poverty. Allah himself smiles on those who do."

Something moved within me when I heard his words. I had known about Uthman Al Ghani all my life, and I'd seen generosity on display in my father's actions. But somehow I had never thought of poverty as something we Muslims had to struggle against. I knew generosity was good, but until that moment, I had not realized just how important it was. If I embraced generosity with the same passion as Uthman Al Ghani, I believed that I, too, might receive a great reward in heaven.

I wasted no time. I began by giving all my pocket money to local widows and orphans, and after a few weeks of doing that, I was hungry for more. I decided to take the expensive gold jewelry my father had bought me and sell every last piece of it. Every rupee went to a local widow.

My parents were proud, but their joy had a limited effect on me. While their blessing was a good thing here on earth, what I really wanted was the assurance that my future in heaven was secure. My mother's smile and my father's stiff nod of approval were no match for the fear within me.

†

Though our street was full of upper middle-class families like mine, the neighborhood was diverse. I only had to walk a few blocks to find beggars and street sweepers, and there was a knot of children from poor backgrounds who spent their days playing in the streets when they weren't working at home. Many of these children were orphans, and all of them were too poor to pay the registration fee and buy the notebooks and pencils required to go to school.

Most people ignored these children. But I could not. The more time I spent with them, the more pity I felt for them. I had known them all by name for years, ever since I joined the state school and fought my way through a mountain of homework every day. I would sit outside on the flat roof of our home with an open book on my lap when I wanted a break. The children would stand beside me, asking what I was reading and pointing out any letters they recognized.

When my mother heard about my interactions with these children, she told me that it reminded her of her own childhood. She had wanted to go to school, but her father refused. So every day when her brothers returned home with their books and sat down to study, she would sit beside them, pestering them with questions. She did not stop until she learned to read.

This gave me an idea. I thought about asking my father for assistance, but I knew he saw little value in education and would not have any interest in my educating the poor. Anwar, however, was more than happy to help. He arranged for a box of textbooks, notebooks, and pencils to be delivered from the madrassa. As soon as the materials arrived, I informed the children that if they wanted to study, I would meet them in the courtyard in front of my house every day after I finished school.

I was careful to call it tutoring rather than school. I did not want to give my father reason to shut it down, and I also knew I could not offer the children all the education they needed. Calling it school would raise its profile, raise their hopes, and put too much pressure on me. It was better to keep things simple.

The sessions were basic. Each day we would meet for thirty minutes and work through two pages of either math and English or science and Urdu. I made sure we all broke to pray when the sun was starting to set, and if any of my eight students were late, I would adopt the sternest expression I could manage, tap my wooden ruler on my hand, and warn them not to be late again. They never were.

†

"What's the best thing you have? Give it to Allah."

Those words from the lips of the mullah were the only ones I heard on a particular Friday afternoon. As soon as he uttered them, my mind latched on to the memory of the day I gave away my gold. I counted down the minutes until I was able to leave the daras, head upstairs, and open my closet. I pushed aside all the dresses that were hanging up and grabbed the one I wanted—the white dress with the intricate embroidery I had spent so much time making. It was beautiful, and I'd been saving it for the day when I finally got my mother to agree that I could wear it. It was the best thing I had.

I took the dress straight to the home of one of the children I taught. My student's mother was a widow with five daughters and one son, and they were poorer than most. My father bought them lentils and oil from time to time and so did other people in the neighborhood, so the mother was used to receiving charity. But when I told her that I was giving it to her daughter, she refused.

"It's too much," she said. "Everybody knows how hard you worked on that dress. Your mother often talks about it with pride. I can't let you give it away."

After more urging on my part, she accepted the dress, and I returned home feeling good. My mother smiled when I told her what I had done, and she agreed that surely Allah had seen me.

As I lay in bed that night, I remembered the day I'd given away my gold jewelry, and I slipped into an idle fantasy about receiving a better dress in return for the one I had given away.

I knew it was foolish, but I couldn't help feeling excited as I got up the next morning and opened my closet. Would I find that I had been rewarded again? Might there be a beautiful white wedding dress, just like the ones I had seen in magazines, waiting for me?

There wasn't, of course, and I spent the rest of the day feeling disappointed—partly with Allah, but mainly with myself. How could I have let myself become distracted by such a childish fantasy?

If I were being completely honest with myself, I would have to admit there was another reason for my increase in generosity. Some months earlier, my father had announced that it was time for me to get married. Neither of my older sisters had attended high school, and both were married when they were still sixteen. As far as my father was concerned, seventeen was far too old for me to be single.

The pressure was on. If I had any hope that my father wouldn't marry me off to some random man who tried to impress him, I needed to be the perfect daughter. If I failed, he would see me as just another problem to be solved as quickly as possible by marrying me off.

I had to make him proud, and to do that, I needed to be the most devout, studious, and generous girl in the city. He already knew I was generous, but that was not enough. He barely paid me any attention, so how was I going to convince him of my other attributes? How could I change his mind if his eyes rarely ever fell on me?

My sky had two moons: the fear of eternal damnation and the fear of losing what little control I had over my earthly life. These twin struggles became the two dominant forces in my life. Yet to my dismay, the harder I strived, the worse I felt.

7

I was still a child when I first saw my father beat my mother. Patches of skin were visible through his wispy beard, which meant he hadn't been with the militants for long. But it took only a few weeks of indoctrination for him to change. Gone was the man who wore Western pants and snuck out to the movies. Gone, too, was the man who allowed his wife to berate him in front of his children.

In his place was a man who stood holding a glass in one hand and my mother's neck in the other. His face was twisted in rage, and flecks of spit were flying out of his mouth. I don't remember what he was shouting about or how the argument began. But I remember pressing against my sisters as we looked out from the kitchen, watching the events unfold in the hallway. I remember the sound the glass made as he brought it down on the side of her head, how its violence and its volume surprised me. And I remember the noise my mother made as she fell to the floor, as if all the life were leaving her body through that tiny whimper.

The next day, after my mother returned from the hospital, I saw that the hair above her ear had been shaved, and her skin was swollen and stitched. From that time forward, things changed at home. My parents' arguments flared more readily, although they often ended just as quickly when my father reminded my mother what would happen if she didn't back down. Sometimes, though, no matter how loudly and desperately she pleaded, his fingers still reached for her throat.

Perhaps I was too young to see it, or maybe I was blind to the truth, but at the time I never made the connection between my father's conversion to militant Islam and the increase in violence in our home. I was unaware of the way the group spread their poison, of how they encouraged my father to embrace his power to lead and rule his family the way a "true" Muslim man should. To my mind, the pain and fear he introduced to our house had nothing to do with his faith. It was simply the way things were.

And that is why, the second time I heard a mullah stand up in the daras and teach about jihad, I did not associate it with violence and fear. Though it wasn't as exciting as the day I gave away my gold jewelry, once again I accepted everything I heard. But now the stakes were even higher. Jihad was not just a matter of how you lived. It was about way more than that. *Yes,* I thought. *This is the way I must die.*

†

I could tell from the number of shoes lined up outside the meeting room that the daras was well attended that Friday afternoon. I took up my usual place beside my mother in the screened-off area and listened as a mullah I had never heard before began to preach.

"This world is your examination hall," he said. "If you pass in this hall, you will have everlasting life. If you pass here, then on the day of judgment you will go to heaven. If you fail, you will go to hell. Every time you face something you think you can't do, remember this truth. Your actions are being recorded and will be remembered on the day of your death."

I remembered my dream from years earlier, the one in which an angel dragged me to hell. I knew all about our deeds being recorded and counted for or against us on the day of our death. But the idea of the world as our examination hall was entirely new to me. It stuck in my chest like a fish bone.

"When we die, what awaits us is the pain of the grave." I knew all about that, too. My mother had often spoken of the way our graves will stretch and pull, crushing and straining us within them. I'd always shivered at the thought.

"But not everybody will face the grave. Those who die for Allah will avoid hell entirely. Anyone who gives their life in jihad will go straight to heaven, straight to paradise. We should all embrace the struggle for that life rather than this one. Brothers and sisters, I tell you that this life is only temporary. Everyone has to die sometime."

†

At first I'd thought of jihad simply as a struggle against poverty. The tools I used in the fight against injustice were my gifts of jewelry and my lovely white dress, and my devotion to educating children who were too poor to attend school. But I knew this was not enough. I had been sensing this for months.

My unease started soon after I gave away the dress. I was still upset about the whole episode—partly with Allah but mainly with myself—when my mother told me that the next daras would not be held at our house.

"Why not?"

"Auntie Selma has asked that we meet at her house."

We had been meeting for weekly gatherings in our home for years, and a special bond had grown between the hundred or so people who attended. Having spent so much time learning about the Qur'an together, encouraging each other to become better Muslims, we had become like family. We helped each other when times were hard and celebrated when times were good. Whenever one of our members had something significant to announce, we often relocated the daras to their home.

Auntie Selma was not an aunt by blood or marriage, but she was special to everyone in the neighborhood. Her husband and three sons were good Muslims—always generous, kind, and devout.

"Has one of her sons gotten engaged?"

"Perhaps," my mother said. "She said she wants all of us to dress up and share a feast."

When Friday finally came, I was excited and decided not to stage another fashion battle with my mother. I gladly chose a dress I knew she liked. We walked the short distance to Auntie Selma's house as a family, my father and brother striding ahead, my mother, sisters, and me following respectfully behind.

Auntie Selma directed the women to one room as her eldest son invited the men into another. "Welcome," she said to the women once we were all inside and the door was closed. She was holding a large photograph of her husband, and suddenly it struck me that months had passed since I'd last seen him.

"My husband has been martyred." Her voice was strong,

and her eyes swept the room as she spoke. "It was his wish that his eldest son should be sent to fight. So next week, I will send him for jihad. You must all pray that he doesn't become fearful and return home, and that when he goes, he fulfills his father's wish. Pray that he will become a martyr too."

The room instantly filled with cries about the greatness of Allah. Auntie Selma stood and smiled as she acknowledged the women's exclamations. Before long we were eating sweets and fragrant rice and drinking cool sodas. The women were buzzing from conversation to conversation. I sat quietly and watched, knowing that this was a place for mothers, not children.

After we returned home, I tried to speak with my mother about this news, quizzing her about where Auntie Selma's husband's jihad had taken place and how he had died. But my mother told me she knew nothing more than what Auntie Selma had said.

Her words did not satisfy my curiosity, and she knew it.

"We might never know how or where he died," she explained to me later that evening. "But we do know for sure that he is a hero. What he did is an example to us all."

8

A few weeks after we heard about the martyrdom, the daras once more relocated to Auntie Selma's house. Again she greeted the women and girls, and again she held a photograph. This time it was her eldest son—the same one who had escorted the men to a different room last time.

"Allah be praised!" she said, her face aglow. "My eldest son went for jihad. He, too, has been martyred. It is just as his father wished."

The cries of joy and praise were even louder this time. Once again there was good food to eat, sodas to drink, and the news that soon, if Allah willed it, Auntie Selma's second son would be sent to jihad, just like his father and brother before him.

The same process repeated itself a month later, and a fourth time the month after that. By then, news of Auntie Selma's family had spread. In addition to the usual attendees of our daras, other people from the city joined us, along with female clerics from the group. They all praised her sons and husband, speaking more highly of them than I'd heard anyone spoken of before.

"My son has made me proud," Auntie Selma said as she held up a photograph. It was different from the ones she had shown us of her husband and other two sons. Those had been the portraits taken after her sons' graduations, where the men looked straight at the camera, full of strength and pride. Her third son's picture, however, showed a bloodied corpse lying on the side of the road.

"He died a martyr's death, and I'm happy," she said. "Now it's my turn. I will go for jihad."

And that was the last I saw of Auntie Selma. By the time the daras met at my family's house the next week, Auntie Selma's property was already empty and boarded up. Not long after that, I heard that she, too, had died. She left her home and all her jewelry to the militants.

For weeks, Auntie Selma was the chief topic of conversation among us women and girls. She was praised for her generosity and held up as an example for us to give without reservation to Allah's cause. She was someone we all admired, and the fact that she, as a woman, had given her life, just as her husband and sons had, gave me a particular thrill.

Her sacrifice taught me that it is possible to give everything for Allah, even if you are a woman.

A change took place within me. Ever since Auntie Selma had left the city, I started seeing my own attempts at generosity in a different light. Giving away a few possessions or teaching for half an hour in the afternoons was nothing compared to what she and her family had done.

Since nobody talked about where or how Auntie Selma's

family had been martyred, I filled in the gaps myself. I had assumed they'd all gone to the border with India, joining the army and fighting in a minor skirmish. Auntie Selma's sons were all young men in their twenties, strong and full of energy, and it was easy to imagine them and their father driving tanks and serving alongside other soldiers. I could even picture Auntie Selma handling a rifle, keeping her nerve as she tended the sick on the battle lines. But I could not see myself in any of these scenarios. I was a quiet eighteen-year-old who loved science and math. I could hardly imagine picking up an AK-47 and marching alongside seasoned troops.

†

As I was sitting next to my mother in the daras one day, a new mullah I had never seen before stood up to speak. And the longer he spoke, the more I understood how wrong I had been. Jihad was not just for men or for the strong and agile; it was for everyone—even girls like me. It was as if a veil were being lifted from my eyes.

"In this battle, we are not fighting for ourselves but for Allah," the mullah said. "You are the army of Allah, not the army of Pakistan. You are here with a job to do and an enemy to fight. Are you willing? Are you prepared to give the life that Allah gave you back to him? Will you take up the weapons Allah provides? It's with rifles and bombs that we fight against the infidel, who would seek to murder and maim our people. That's how we will remove America from the face of the earth!"

At that, the room filled with shouts of support and cries of "Allahu Akbar!"

The mullah went on, his voice rising in volume and pitch. "Is it not true that Allah rewards those who serve him? I tell you the truth: the more infidels you kill, the greater your reward will be. Allah will see how many Christians and Jews you destroy, and he will not forget. And for those who give their lives in jihad, their family will also be given the same reward in paradise. No grave, no judgment—just straight to paradise. Think of those seventy-two virgins your father will be given because of you! And remember those pillows that will be so soft, and the walls of the garden so high. Would you not be proud to give such riches to your mother?"

By now the room was thick with excitement. But I sat in silence, my eyes closed tight. So much of what he said was familiar, like the fact that the only way to guarantee our entry to heaven was to give our life in jihad. But there was one thing the mullah said that I had never heard before: the idea that I could get my parents a place in heaven without having to face the trial of judgment.

It was a promise so marvelous that my lungs felt like they were filling with the sweetest of air. I pictured myself in heaven, welcoming my father as he stared in amazement at the home in paradise I had secured for him.

"You did this for me?" he would say.

"Yes," I would reply. "I did it for you. Me, the daughter you refused to see. Me, the daughter who has brought you into paradise."

He would stand and stare for a moment, his eyes locked on mine. He might cry, perhaps even sob. Eventually he would open his arms and embrace me. For the first time in my life, I would know what it felt like to be safe in my father's arms.

†

"Are there any volunteers for jihad?" the mullah asked at the end of the meeting.

I held my hand up high. The room had fallen into a reverent silence as he waited for other hands to be raised, but I didn't even notice the people around me. My head was full of noise.

It was only when I felt my mother's hand rest softly on my back that I remembered she was next to me. Her hand felt warm. I opened my eyes to look at her, and through her veil, I could see that her eyes were wet with tears.

I looked around me. I was the only one on the women's side of the curtain with my hand raised, and all eyes were on me.

The meeting ended soon after, and the mullah told me to sit and wait while he spoke with the men who had volunteered. Instead of listening to what he was saying to the men, I sat there wondering where this jihad might take me. Perhaps I would be sent to fight on the border with India. Perhaps I, too, would be called on to give my life in battle. I was not nervous or worried. I was simply determined. Whatever it cost me, if it brought my father and mother with me to paradise, it would be worth it.

When the mullah finally appeared before me, I looked at him properly for the first time that day. He was younger than most clerics, and his eyes were kind.

When he spoke to me, his voice was gentler than it had been during the daras. "I'm so happy that you're going to give your life. But you must remember that this fight is not for ourselves but for Islam. We fight to save Islam, just as Muhammad and the caliphs did. They all fought and gave their lives. They were all martyred. I don't want you to think about the moment you will die. It will be very quick. I want you to think about the reward that awaits you in heaven. You will hear the sound of waterfalls, and whatever you want will be yours as soon as you think of it. Any clothes, any kind of food—all of it will be yours. Your next life will be so much better than this one. It sounds good, doesn't it?"

"Yes," I said. "It does."

"So don't worry about anything. We'll teach you everything you need to know—how to use a rifle, how to wear the suicide vest, and how to detonate it. You'll need to be careful to kill as many infidels as you can. Remember that the more you kill, the bigger your reward will be. So we'll help you learn how to pick the biggest crowd."

"But what if there are Muslims among them?" I asked, feeling anxious for the first time. "What will Allah do to me then?"

"Don't worry about that, either. Theirs will be a martyr's death, just like yours. They'll go to heaven, just as you will. You'll save many lives this way. Do you have any more questions?"

I had thousands, but none I could ask. Anwar had been clear about how important it was not to think too deeply about the Qur'an. Perhaps the mullah would say the same thing to me now. Thinking would only make things worse.

The mullah got ready to leave. "We'll call you in two months, when we're ready for the next wave of recruits. Then we'll take you to the camp and train you. You won't see your family in this life again after you leave, so use these weeks well."

We said good-bye, and I stayed in the meeting room, listening to the crowd drift away from the courtyard. I watched the way the sunlight tracked across the room, growing ever softer as it did.

It felt strange to have committed to something so momentous, to have made such a significant decision on an ordinary Friday afternoon.

"Everyone has to die sometime," I said quietly. The familiarity of the words reassured me. I believed them, and I was ready for that day to be sooner rather than later.

After the meeting, I was surrounded by jubilant women. They clasped my hands and exclaimed over me, whispering their blessings as they left. It was a time to celebrate—that was clear. But I did not feel full of joy. I felt the way I did when I realized there was no way Allah was going to provide me with a replacement dress for the one I had given away. I was humbled, yes. But unburdened as well. I had been foolish to think that a dress would appear in my closet, and I'd been just as foolish to believe I could be generous or devout enough to win either my father's affection or Allah's rewards.

Everyone has to die sometime.

At least this way I knew my death would be worth something.

Part 2

YOU WILL
BE HATED BY
EVERYONE

9

My father was delighted that his daughter would be engaging in jihad—so delighted that the subject of my marriage was dropped. Not that he ever said this to my face. He and I were hardly ever in the same room, let alone in a position to have a real conversation about marriage, jihad, or anything else. But I knew he was happy—my mother told me so.

If my mother felt differently, she hid it well. Right from the moment I volunteered for jihad, a close bond had formed between us, even closer than usual. She'd laid her hand on my back as soon as I volunteered, and in many ways, it felt as though she had never removed it.

She and I had always spent a lot of time together, whether it was in the workshop or cooking together in the kitchen. My mother did not play favorites, but there was no denying she had a closer relationship with me than she did with my other siblings. My two elder sisters had both married and left home by this time. My younger brother was seventeen and had always been the apple of my father's eye. My younger sister was close to everyone in our house—to both of our parents as well as to my brother, me, and the two women who came every day to clean the house. For reasons I was never able to understand, she was free in ways I could only dream of being.

"I don't want you to worry," my mother said one morning not long after the daras. "You remember what I always tell you, don't you?"

"Everyone has to die sometime?"

"Yes. Maybe tomorrow I will die too. What would happen to me then? I would face judgment. Would my good deeds outweigh my bad? Or what if I died while I was unclean? Nothing could save me then. Isn't it better for you to die this way, with no husband and no children, knowing you are doing Allah's work and you will be swept straight into paradise? We are all born in Islam; we have to die in Islam. When you give this life for Allah, it is no loss—only a benefit."

I heard nothing from the militants in the weeks following the daras. As time passed, I almost forgot what I'd agreed to. I concentrated on my studies, started a new sewing project, and struggled to help some of the orphans understand calculus. I felt good—almost at peace.

There was no hatred in me. I did not sign up for jihad because I despised America or because I wanted to kill Christians and Jews. As far as I knew, I had never met a Christian or a Jew. I even admired them a little—or at least I admired the tools and machines and medicines they'd given the world.

Of course, I had not forgotten the lessons from the madrassa about how Christians and Jews persecuted Muslims and how they'd killed my people so brutally in Bosnia, Chechnya, and

Palestine. But even so, I didn't raise my hand out of hatred. I chose jihad because of Allah. I chose it because of love. I chose it because I was desperate for my father's approval.

†

My mother was standing in the courtyard when I returned home from school one afternoon. Two months had passed, and even before she spoke, I knew what she was going to say.

"They called. They will come to collect you next week."

For the briefest moment, I felt relieved. It felt like the instant a match flares and catches flame—a burst of emotion, a flood of good feeling. At last, the waiting was over. The end was about to begin.

But when I woke early the next morning and walked through the house to begin my first prayers of the day, whatever peace I'd experienced the day before faded. My limbs felt heavy; my stomach twisted as if it were gripped by an invisible vice.

The feelings of dread grew stronger throughout the day.

Somehow, during the two months of waiting, I had forgotten that when I left for jihad training, I would never again return home. Every time I looked at the things around me, from the guava trees in the courtyard to the rickshaws that filled the city streets, I wondered how many more times I'd see them before I died.

I tried to tell myself not to think this way. After all, dwelling on such things would only make me weak. So all through the day, I dug my fingernails into my palms, forcing myself to picture the next life and how beautiful it would be. It almost worked, but as soon as I came back home and saw my trophies on my shelf or the family photos on the wall, the questions came back louder than ever.

Will they remember me? Will they miss me? Will it be as if I never existed?

The only thing I could do was pray.

For well over two years, I'd been offering prayers eight times a day. There were no new prayers to be said, no extra rituals to observe. So I made the prayers last longer. What usually took me ten minutes I'd spin out for an hour. I took extra care as I washed and prepared myself and then repeated every prayer until my mouth felt too dry to speak. I clung to my prayer mat as if it were a life raft and I were alone in the middle of the ocean.

My relationship with my mother was changing too. Her health was deteriorating, resulting in periods of fatigue and breathlessness, but there was more to it than that. Her attitude toward me shifted. She held my hand more often than usual and offered to take me anywhere I wanted to go. She even said she'd cook me anything I requested to eat. I knew that I was going to die. Would she be far behind?

"I don't need anything," I said every time she offered me food, keeping hold of her hand. "I just want to stay here with you."

I thought a lot about Auntie Selma during that week. Had she felt as apprehensive as I did? I couldn't imagine that she did. She seemed so brave and strong, so happy to be giving her life in jihad. So I did what I thought she would have done and prayed some more. Better to spend time with Allah than to waste my last few days at home eating or walking around the city.

Yet I still felt no peace. Despite the mullah's promises, I felt sure Allah would cast me away. Even if I somehow took the lives of one hundred infidels, I could not imagine him granting me the kind of riches the mullah said would be mine.

As I prayed, I tried to picture myself kneeling before him, just as I had done before Anwar. Only Allah would be on the throne, and instead of begging for the chance to go to school, I'd be begging for the chance to remain in heaven. I would beg him to show me mercy, to allow me to remain with him. I did not need a mansion with soft, white pillows or a garden with high walls. If Allah would only let me stay with him, I wouldn't care how humble a corner of heaven I was given. That would be enough.

†

I woke to the sound of the *azan*, the call for the world to pray. I knew that nobody else in the house would answer it. My mother was too weak, my siblings were too comfortable in their beds, and my father . . . well, I could not remember ever seeing him up to pray at 3:30 a.m. I was glad of it too. I could not imagine sharing the prayer room with only him.

I had been getting up with the cockerels for so long that I was barely conscious as I moved. I slipped out of my room, past my sleeping little sister, and along the corridor to the bathroom. How many more times would I get up for morning prayers before I was gone? And where would I be taken? Would it be far from the city? Would it look like a military camp or a school yard?

I told myself that I wasn't scared or troubled. I told myself that I was ready. *I could die in an accident tomorrow,* I thought. *I could get knocked down in the street, and what good would that do me? Better to die and receive Allah's rewards than to die and face his judgment.*

In the bathroom, however, I saw something that drained my confidence. Blood. Starting my menstrual cycle meant that I was unclean. Unclean Muslims could not touch the

Qur'an, pray, or even touch their prayer mat. I also assumed that unclean Muslims could not go to heaven, and they certainly couldn't start jihad training.

I was troubled—too troubled to go back to bed—so I continued on to the prayer room. Sitting on the floor, with my mat rolled up beside me, I felt a deep sorrow growing within me. I slouched onto the floor, too sad to do anything else for a while.

I wondered whether, since my tongue was still clean, Allah might listen if I prayed to him in my own language, Urdu, rather than Arabic. "O my Creator, in a few days I will be going for jihad training. I am giving my life to you because you have created me. Please, I'm begging you, don't send me to the fires of hell on judgment day."

The words were like dirt in my mouth. How could I talk to Allah as if he were just another person in the room with me? How could I hope to barter with him like this?

As I was praying, my mind began to drift. I wondered about heaven and hell, and whether Allah would be merciful if I, an unclean woman, were to die at that very moment. Where would Allah send me? Had I done enough?

Soon I was dreaming. In my dream, I was in a graveyard. I knew that I had died and my death had not been a glorious act of jihad. Terror coursed through me—I was afraid I would step on the graves and hurt the people still trapped in them. Everything around me was soaked in darkness—I could practically taste it. I was desperate to leave and searched in vain for a way out.

"Allah!" I called out in Urdu. "Please be merciful!"

I kept searching for an exit but stopped when I saw a single light appear in front of me, a little ways off. The closer the light came, the more clearly I could see. It shone brighter than anything I had ever seen. It was like the sun in full blaze, yet somehow I could look at it. As the light came closer, I saw that it had a face, hands, and feet. It was not just a light; it was a person. A man. And he was speaking to me.

"Come and follow me."

"No!" I replied.

"Esther, come and follow me."

The name this man used confused me. "I'm sorry," I told the man made of light, "but I'm not Esther. I am Zakhira Ahmad, and I don't want to follow you."

The voice was softer when it spoke for a third time. The warmth and love that flowed with the words spread deep into my skin. "My daughter, come and follow me."

I couldn't say no a third time. I didn't *want* to say no. I wanted to live in that voice, to inhale those words and float on them forever. As I breathed, it dawned on me that perhaps this person in my dream might actually be able to help get me out of the graveyard. Why was he calling me his daughter? I had no idea, but I decided to do as he said.

As soon as I made that decision, the light started moving through the graveyard. I stood, transfixed, and watched his feet as he went. Every bush and stone on the path in front of him was swept away by invisible hands as soon as he approached. Wherever he stepped, the darkness faded away. And he left behind a trail of light—and not just light, but life.

Oh! I said to myself. *This light really is showing me the way out.* I started to chase after him, running along the path, which was now flooded with light. When he stopped in front of a grave, I stood at his side.

"Come out," he said, looking into the grave. I watched, amazed, as a dead man immediately rose out of the earth. Under other circumstances, I would not have been able to take my eyes off the resurrected body, but in the dream, all I cared about was the man made of light.

"Who are you to be giving life to dead people?" I asked.

He turned to me. I could feel the light deep in my lungs. "I am the way, the truth, and the life," he said.

"Please, help me." My voice sounded small. "I want to get out of this graveyard."

He put his hand around mine. The moment he touched me, the graveyard fell away. In its place was a sight of beauty the likes of which I had never seen before. In front of us lay an ocean of brilliant light—but solid, as if it were made of crystal. Beside us and behind us was a building whose walls were made of gold. But this was not the sort of gold I had seen in even the finest jewelry. That kind of gold was lifeless and frail, while these walls were full of life and power and light.

When I was younger, I would sometimes turn on the tap in the bathroom and listen, enchanted, to the sound the water made as it filled up the sink. In my dream, I heard that same sound nearby, only this time it felt as though I could hear it with every cell in my body.

The light was equally all-encompassing. Everything around me wasn't just bathed in light; it *was* light. The crystal ocean, the golden walls, even the waterfall that was hidden from my view—they all seemed to pulse with light. It was as if my eyes were seeing for the very first time.

The view before me was beyond anything I had ever seen, beyond anything I could imagine. I needed all my senses to take it in. I tried desperately to hold it in my mind, to go deeper into it, to understand what this place was.

Then I woke up.

The prayer room was silent. The air was still. I looked around me, reminding myself of my surroundings by looking at the familiar objects: the pile of rolled-up prayer mats, the cupboard filled with copies of the Qur'an, the window that looked out onto the courtyard. I was at home. Where I belonged.

And yet I suddenly felt like this was not home—that there was somewhere else I longed for at the core of my being. I had received a taste of something I'd been craving for years but had never found.

For the first time in my life, I felt peace.

10

As I got my bearings after waking up in the prayer room, I realized my mother was kneeling beside me in prayer. I listened as she recited the words that were as familiar to me as the threads of my own prayer mat. She finished, gently stroked my arm, and left in silence.

In the light of morning, the dream was as real to me as it had been a few hours earlier. So, too, was the feeling of peace that had settled inside me ever since the man of light had spoken to me in the graveyard.

I did not like it.

Why would I feel peaceful when I had been dreaming about a graveyard—a place that everyone knows is unclean? Graveyards are never good places for Muslims to be, so why was I there?

And why would I dream of light? Surely the light was a good sign, but would something good be found somewhere so unclean?

I remembered the fear I had experienced at the beginning of the dream—how it felt like the darkness would consume me. But then the man made of light called that dead person out of the grave. How was that even possible? Why did he call me "Daughter," and what was that place he took me to?

Perhaps the thing that troubled me most was the dream itself. If it was from Allah, why would he send it to me when I was unclean?

It was all too much. The questions gnawed at my mind like fleas in a bedsheet. I wanted them to go away. They did not seem like the sorts of questions a good Muslim would be asking a few days before she went off to fight jihad.

And yet the peace remained. In spite of the dream and the knowledge that I was only four days away from leaving my family forever, I still felt at peace.

†

Thanks to Anwar's support, my father had consented to my enrolling in college. My grades hadn't been good enough for medicine, but I had made it into a pre-engineering course at a local university. I was enjoying my studies, though the morning of my dream, I was too unsettled to eat breakfast before I made the long walk across the city to my classes. All the traffic and people were welcome distractions from the chaos in my mind.

Unlike most days, I didn't find myself looking sadly at the familiar trees on my route or wondering how long it would be before my fellow students forgot about me. I quickly made my way to my first lesson and waited for the physics practical to start.

"Hello, Zakhira," Azia said as she sat next to me. I did not know her well, but I always looked forward to killing time with her in idle conversation while we waited for the lecturer.

That day the conversation was anything but idle.

"Are you okay?" Azia asked.

"Yes. Why?" I was obviously flustered.

"You don't look like you usually do. You look different."

I tried my best to brush her off, explaining that I was just tired from an early morning. She smiled and opened her book.

By the time the lesson began and Azia and I started our work together, my mind was once again flooded with questions. All morning I had been able to hold them back, but one comment from Azia was enough to break the whole dam.

I worried that if Azia could tell something was different about me, others would notice too. I'd be rejected from the jihad camp, and not only would I fail to secure my and my family's position in paradise, but I would bring shame on my parents for failing to fight fully for Allah.

Most of all, I could not stop thinking about the light. What was it? Who was it? I didn't think he was an angel, because he had no wings on his back. And I knew Allah wouldn't show himself to any human being, since humans are lowly. What did he mean when he said he was the way, the truth, and the life? That strange phrase made no sense to me. Surely any messenger from Allah would have simply declared, "I am of Allah." And why was Allah sending me a messenger at all, when I was about to die anyway?

The most powerful image from the dream was the place where the light had taken me. Was that what heaven looked like? There were no high-walled gardens or soft, ivory-white pillows, but it looked even more beautiful than I'd ever imagined.

"Zakhira!" Azia nudged me in the ribs, warning me too late to stop my precarious tower of books from toppling over and crashing to the floor. The whole class turned to look at me.

"What's the matter today?" Azia whispered as I rearranged my side of the table.

"Nothing," I said automatically. Then I thought better of it. "I had a strange dream last night." I hoped that if I said it out loud, the dream would lose some of its power.

Azia wasn't satisfied. "Really? What happened in it?"

I sighed. "It was nothing, really. Just one of those strange dreams."

Azia let it go for a while but soon leaned in close and lowered her voice. "You seem troubled by it, though. Would you let me pray for you? Whenever I'm worried about something, I try to pray. It helps."

I knew all the eight prayers by heart, and none of them fit what she described. They were all about Allah's power and judgment, not about our worries and weaknesses. "What kind of prayer do you pray?"

"It's a Christian prayer."

I recoiled. I had no idea Azia was a Christian—her name was a common enough Muslim name, and she wore a dupatta like the rest of us. I had never really met a Christian before, but I knew all about them. My mother had told me that they had rewritten the Bible, changing it from its original version. They could not be trusted, and they performed black magic. As far as I was concerned, I would do whatever I could to avoid them.

"I don't want you to pray for me at all," I said. "I'm not interested in your black magic. I'm a Muslim, remember?"

"I know," she said, her voice cracking. "We can pray for Muslims, too."

"Not me. I don't want anything like that from you—do you understand?"

When the practical was finished, I left before Azia could

say another word. My walk home from college was much worse than my trip there. Instead of being a distraction, the rickshaws and crowds were an unwelcome manifestation of all the thoughts that were crowding in on me.

When I arrived at home, I refused the food my mother offered me. I saw my group of students for their usual afternoon tutoring, but my mind was an ocean away from the pages we were working through. Afterward I sat alone in the prayer room and then walked up to the rooftop to look out at the setting sun. Everywhere I went, everything I did, the questions swirled within me, closer than the breath in my lungs.

Why did I have this dream?

What does it mean?

And why do I feel this strange peace?

†

When I arrived at class the next day, I made sure I was early. I didn't want to see Azia and run the risk of her offering to pray for me again. I took my place in the lecture hall, tucking myself away in a corner and hiding my head in a book.

My heart sank when I sensed someone approaching. Even before I looked up, I knew it was Azia.

"Can you come outside? I want to talk to you."

"No." I tried to fill my voice with the kind of strength that would communicate how serious I was but not attract attention from anyone else. "I'm waiting for class to start."

"But I have something I want to give you."

I shook my head firmly, glared at her, and went back to my book.

Azia sat next to me. Were all Christians this unstoppable? She held a canvas bag in front of her, her hands grasping the handles tightly, as if whatever was inside was either fragile or extremely dangerous. "I brought these for you," she whispered. "It's some books and a cassette. I think they might help you understand your dream."

"What books?"

She looked right at me, her mouth twitching. When she finally spoke, her voice was so quiet I could barely hear her. "One of them is part of the Bible."

A wave of anger surged within me. "I don't want them!" I spit out my words like knives. "Did I ask you to bring any books in for me? Did I ask you to pray for me?"

"No," she said, "but I—"

"Listen to me! I'm not interested in whatever you have in that bag. Everybody knows that the Bible has been changed anyway. Why would you think I'd be interested in reading it?"

Azia looked away for a moment. The lecture hall was filling up, and people were starting to file into the chairs nearby. When she looked back at me, her eyes were wet and her voice was shaking with fear. "Please, Zakhira. For me, just take them. If you don't want them, you can bring them back tomorrow. I promise I'll take them back."

Her fear reminded me of my own.

"Okay," I said. "Put them in my bag."

†

As I sat in my room later that day, having carefully placed the books and cassette at the back of my closet, it struck me that Azia was the first Christian I'd ever had a conversation with. Part of me was intrigued. I was surprised that I hadn't known about her faith, and I admired her courage.

Another part of me was repelled by Azia. The things my mother had told me about Christians had impacted me deeply.

And I could not forget the images I had seen years earlier when I attended the madrassa. Yet somehow I couldn't imagine Azia hurting one of my Muslim brothers or sisters. She was far too gentle for that.

The house was empty. For a moment I thought about reaching into the closet and reading one of the books Azia had given me. What would I find in the Bible? Would it help explain my dream? Might it give me the answers I was looking for?

My thoughts stopped dead.

What was I thinking? I was three days away from being taken for jihad, and I was already worried enough that menstruating made me unclean. How fierce would the rage of Allah be if I let my mind be seduced by the lies of an infidel?

I reached for the books and the cassette and ran to the kitchen, my hands tearing up the pages without even looking at them. I didn't want to infect myself in any way. I worked fast, nervous that someone would return at any moment. Using the mortar and pestle, which smelled of garlic and ginger, I used all my strength to crush the cassette. When the bowl was a mess of plastic shards and crinkled black tape, I carefully scooped it all into the trash, along with the ripped-up pages of the books. I was careful to bury all of it deep beneath the kitchen scraps.

As I left the kitchen, I saw a piece of paper on the floor just as someone was opening the front door. I hid the page in my dress and went back upstairs.

Later that night, I took some matches to the bathroom and burned the page from the Bible in front of an open window. My hand was shaking as I held it. As the last embers lost their glow and the thin line along the edge faded from red to black, I thought about Anwar. What would he say if he saw me now? Would he smile at me, offering gentle encouragement?

If so, why did burning the page like that feel somehow wrong, even dangerous?

I brushed the final pieces out the window and hoped my mother was right about the Bible being distorted. If not, I feared there was even more trouble to come.

11

My mother's cries woke me up the next morning. The call to prayer followed soon after, but it was the sound of my mother in pain that stirred me to action. Her heart condition had caused her discomfort for years, but recently her health had declined even further. I often found her curled up on her bed in pain or pausing, breathless, midway through some simple task. Even so, hearing her cry loudly enough to wake the entire house meant that she was experiencing a whole new level of agony.

As the oldest daughter at home, I felt it was my duty to skip college for the day and take my mother to the hospital as soon as possible. She struggled to make it out to the street, and even stepping into the rickshaw left her clutching her side and gasping in pain.

She did not talk much as we slid through the traffic, and I let my thoughts return once more to the plan I had been developing all morning. I decided there was no shame in admitting that my dream had thrown me and that it was impossible for me to ignore the questions it had left me with. It was therefore logical that I give myself some time to work it out.

The jihad training was due to start within forty-eight hours, but if I could delay my departure for a while, I'd be able to think through the dream and suffocate my doubts once and for all. A month should be more than enough.

Even though there were no female surgeons in the area, there was a female doctor on duty at the hospital. After examining my mother carefully, she prescribed painkillers and told her to visit the lab on the second floor to have blood drawn and tested. It was a short walk to the lab, and I had accompanied my mother on this journey more than once before. But this time was different. Her feet shuffled slowly. Every step was a battle.

I entered the lab and found a seat for my mother. Then I called out a traditional Islamic greeting to the man with his head hidden behind a stack of papers: "As-salaam alaikum!"

"Salaam," he replied.

His greeting angered me. "Excuse me?" I marched over to the desk so I could see him more clearly. "Why didn't you greet me properly? Don't you know that you're supposed to reply 'Wa-alaikum salaam' [And may the peace and mercy and blessings of Allah be upon you]? Did you forget, or are you not really a Muslim?"

"No," he said, clasping his hands together in front of his chest and smiling at me. "Thank God, I'm a Christian."

I could not believe it—this was the second Christian I had met in the span of two days. What was going on? I decided not to let that bother me and instead to see this for what it was: an opportunity to put into practice all that Anwar and the other clerics had taught me over the years.

I would be polite and invite him to join Islam. Once I'd made friends with him, he would feel relaxed and trust me. After that I would plant a doubt about Christianity in his mind, and then another. Soon I'd win him over—I was sure of it. And when that happened, I would know that Allah was surely with me and that my reward in heaven was secure.

My veil covered everything but my eyes, so I had to rely on my voice to convey the warm smile I adopted as I spoke. "Well, it would be very good if you accepted Islam. Did you know that Islam is the superior religion all over the world? Wouldn't you like to belong to the very best of all religions?"

The man behind the desk scrunched up his face, as if a bad smell had just entered the room. "What can your Islam possibly give me?"

I ignored his rudeness and kept smiling beneath my veil. "Anything at all! Whatever you want, Islam can give you!" Perhaps if I could take him to see my father, he would understand what I was talking about. If he could see my father's wealth and meet some of the mullahs, he'd understand what it means to live a good Muslim life.

"Can your Islam give me salvation?"

"Yes," I shot back immediately, even though I was not completely sure I understood what salvation was. Was it something like hope? "Anything you want, Islam can give you."

He held my stare for a moment, and then he snorted, dismissed me with a wave of his hand, and returned to his work. "I think you haven't read your Qur'an. Go away and read it properly from now on."

It was impossible to continue to be polite in the face of such rudeness. I gave in to my anger and jabbed a finger at him.

"You're wrong! I've been reading the Qur'an since I was young. I've read it many times."

"Oh really? Have you read Surah Al-Ahqaf?"

"Of course I have," I said, sneering. Everyone had read that section. This man was clearly a fool.

"And you read number 46, Surah Al-Ahqaf?"

"Yes."

"And you are sure that you read verse 9?"

"Of course!"

He said nothing for a while, then shrugged and went back to his papers.

"What?" I said. "You don't believe me?"

"No, I don't. I don't think you've read your Qur'an at all, especially not that verse. It describes Allah instructing Muhammad to say, 'I'm no new thing among the messengers [of Allah], nor know I what will be done with me or with you. I do but follow that which is inspired in me, and I am but a plain Warner.' And you're telling me that Islam can give me salvation? How can it, when even Muhammad admitted that he didn't know what would happen after death?"

I hated to admit it, but his words bothered me. I knew Christians had changed the Bible to remove Muhammad from it. Could it be that this sneaky man had also changed the Qur'an to plant a doubt in my mind?

"Write down the Surah and verse for me," I said. "I'll go home and look it up in my Qur'an. And give me your phone number so I can call you if it's wrong."

He did as I asked and handed me the piece of paper.

"If it's not the same, will you become a Muslim?"

"Yes," he said. And then he gave me a smile of such warmth and confidence that I had to look away. "If the words *are* the same," he said, "will you become a Christian? It's a bold step to take, but I promise you won't regret it."

"No." I shook my head, thinking of the dream and the burned page of the Bible and the jihad camp that was awaiting me. It was all so confusing, but one thing I knew for sure: what he suggested was never going to happen. "That would be impossible. I could never turn my back on Islam. Besides, I'm 110 percent sure you're trying to trick me. There's no way that verse is going to be the same in my Qur'an."

†

My bleeding had stopped that morning. As soon as my mother and I arrived home, I hurried to carry out my cleansing rituals and head to the prayer room. A few minutes later I sat cross-legged on the floor, my Urdu-language copy of the Qur'an open on my lap. The verse was the same as the man at the hospital had said. Word for word.

I felt as though my lungs had been torn from my chest.

All my life I had been brought up to know that Muhammad and Muhammad alone could save us from the wrath of Allah. Yet here was proof that Muhammad didn't even know his own fate, let alone the fate that awaits the rest of us. How could that be? And if Muhammad could not save me, then who could?

The man in the lab had said something to me before I left, and the words came back to me in the prayer room: "If a leader doesn't know what lies ahead, then why follow him? That's like following a blind man down a well."

I went downstairs, told my mother that I was calling the hospital to check on her test results, and pulled out the piece of paper where he had written the verse, his phone number, and his name.

"Is this John?" I said quietly when he answered. "I want to see you tomorrow."

"Ah," he said. "So you read the verse."

"Yes, I read it."

"And was it the same in your Qur'an?"

"Yes, it was."

"You can come tomorrow afternoon. It will be quiet then— we can talk."

The next day in class, I carefully avoided contact with Azia. When the lectures began, my mind was distracted. At times I tried to imagine what John might say to me. At other times I felt fear grip me tight as I wondered what Allah would make of my meeting a Christian. I stumbled through the lessons, my mind a million miles away. It was only when I saw my lecturer in Islamic studies in the courtyard after class that I woke up.

I mentioned to her that I had been reading my Urdu translation of Surah Al-Ahqaf, number 46, and was troubled by verse 9. "What does it mean when Allah tells Muhammad to tell others that he doesn't know what will happen to him?"

She looked at me kindly. "My daughter," she said, "don't read translations of the Qur'an. People who read those translations in search of the true meaning of the words often get confused. Some are even led astray from the right path. It's better to stick to reading it in Arabic. You know that learning each word of the Qur'an in Arabic carries thirty times as great a reward as any other language, don't you? Think of judgment day! Stick to Arabic, and increase your rewards."

A month or even a week earlier, her advice would have spurred me to learn as much of the Qur'an in Arabic as I possibly could. But not now. With John's words ringing in my mind, I found myself unsatisfied by her advice.

As soon as my classes were finished, I made the twenty-minute walk to the hospital. I was glad to see that John was alone in the lab.

I did not bother getting into an argument with him about greetings; instead, I got straight to making my request. "Can I have your book? I want to read it. But don't think I'm going to become a Christian—I just want to know what it has to say."

He sat back in his chair and spread out his hands in front of him. "Well, first, you may not call it 'your book.' It's the Holy Bible. Second, I'm sorry, but I can't give you my Holy Bible. You've made it clear that you have no intention of following Christianity. So please go back home and read your Qur'an properly. Learn how to ask questions of it. Come back when you've done that, and perhaps then I'll be able to give you the Holy Bible."

For a moment I considered arguing, but when I spoke, there was no fight in my voice. "What kind of questions should I ask?"

"Think about everything you've read and learned in your Qur'an until now, and ask yourself, *Am I walking on the right path?* No one else will be answerable to God on your behalf on judgment day."

In that moment the air turned stale, and I felt my chest tightening. Was he talking about me and jihad? Was there any way he could know about that?

"You're clearly an educated person," he continued. "Educated people have brains to think with, ears to hear with, and feelings to aid them as they make their decisions. Educated people can better understand and differentiate between right and wrong. Surely someone who asks questions and doesn't rest until they find answers will find the right path."

Something inside me warmed as I listened to John. With the exception of a few teachers, I'd never had someone speak so

openly and confidently to me before. To hear an educated, pro-
fessional man talk to me this way was something entirely new.

"You know that you can't say to black that it is white or to
night that it is day. You know that you can never follow the
blind, because the blind can't show you the way. Like all educated people, you work hard to discern what is true and real.
I'm sure you will also do this as you examine the Qur'an. Will
you take this challenge?"

"Yes," I said. I liked that he saw me as educated, and I
wanted him to know that I was not afraid to examine my faith.
Perhaps when he saw me explore the Qur'an, it might even
sow a doubt or two in his mind about his Holy Bible.

I was just getting ready to leave when he made his final
comment.

"I'm not against Muslims, and I'm not against your faith
and beliefs. We are cousins, remember. Prophet Abraham had
two sons from different wives: Ishmael and Isaac. We both
descend from their lineage."

As I walked home that afternoon, the sense of peace I had
been feeling grew even stronger. I'd been so convinced that
John would say yes when I asked him for a Bible. After all,
I hadn't even asked Azia for Christian books or tapes, and she
had given me a bag full of materials.

But John was different.

He wasn't at all like the Christians I'd heard described
in the madrassa, and he did not fit my mother's description
either. He wasn't cruel or full of hate; he was friendly and
courteous. The more I listened to him, the more I could feel
myself wanting to trust him. He didn't want me to go on the
wrong path; he hoped I would find the right one.

Surely, I told myself, *if I do what he says, all this confusion
will fade away.*

12

Azia and John were the first Christians I'd ever spoken to, but they were not the first I'd seen. One afternoon before my father had fallen in with the radicals, back when he wore tight Western pants and bright shirts, he received a visitor. My mother was out of the house, and my father told my older sisters to prepare some tea and snacks and to knock on the door when they were ready.

I watched from the window, my face pressed against the glass alongside my sisters, as he greeted a stranger in the courtyard. He was dressed just like my father, but when he came into the house, the difference between them became apparent. The stranger was wearing the most exotic cologne I had ever smelled, and it seemed to me that the air was filled with mystery.

I was too young to know what business this man had with my father, and I didn't think to ask my sisters. I just followed them down to the kitchen and let my nose pick out the strange, sweet scents he introduced.

Soon after my sisters had performed their duties, my mother returned to the house.

"Who's here?" she asked.

All of us girls shrugged and told her that we didn't know who the visitor was. She left us in the kitchen, but from there we could hear her open the door to the drawing room. We heard raised voices, and shortly after, the front door opened and then quickly shut again.

"Why did you do that?" my father asked my mother.

"Because I know who that man is."

"He's a business contact. Whenever he's in town, I always meet up with him."

"Yes," my mother said, "and he's a Christian, isn't he?"

My father said nothing.

"I'm right, aren't I?"

"Yes," he said quietly.

My sisters and I crept toward the doorway of the drawing room just in time to see my mother walk over to the tray that held the drinks and snacks my father had asked for. She picked up the cups and saucers—the best ones that we brought out only for honored guests—and turned to face my father. Then she hurled them to the floor, where they shattered into hundreds of pieces.

"Why?" My father stared at the floor.

"Because a Christian touched them. They were unclean."

†

"Why?"

Whenever my mother looked at me intently like this, it

made me nervous. I had rehearsed my answer a dozen times, but still the words were slow to come.

"Why?" she asked again, a little more gently this time. Was she trying to keep her emotions in check?

"I just want to spend more time with Allah," I said. "I need to pray more."

She looked at me carefully and then smiled. "Okay, I will call them."

I waited on the stairs and listened to her half of the conversation.

"No, there's no problem. She just says she needs more time. . . . Yes, she's praying even more than usual, offering eight prayers a day. . . . She reads her Qur'an too. . . . No, she's not scared. And she hasn't changed her mind. She just needs time to be ready. . . . Yes, I will. As soon as she's ready."

My mother ended the call and walked over to join me on the stairs. She winced with pain as she bent down, but even though I protested and tried to stand up, she was determined to sit beside me.

"They say they're confident you'll be ready soon," she said when she was finally seated. I could feel the silk of her dress on my arm. "I think it's natural to want to wait awhile to make sure you're ready. I'm so happy you're spending time with Allah. You know, people are noticing how dedicated you are, and they're impressed. I tell them that you and Allah are so close."

I had nothing to say in return. Part of me felt relieved that I'd bought myself some time, but part of me was still deeply troubled. Everything felt fragile, as if a mighty storm were coming and I had suddenly discovered that the house was held up by thin sticks. It would only be a matter of time before everything fell down.

†

I set a task for myself: I would approach the Qur'an with the eyes of a scientist. In fact, I wouldn't limit myself to the Qur'an; I'd study the hadith as well, weighing the historical accounts of Muhammad's life and asking questions the way John had suggested.

Like any good scientist, I was testing my hypothesis—that the Qur'an was true and trustworthy, and that the verse John had shown me had somehow been twisted and used incorrectly. I still believed in Muhammad and I still believed in Allah, and once I found the evidence to back up my position, I could go back to John and expose his devious Christian lies.

I was in trouble almost from the very start.

I turned to a story in the Qur'an about a man named Dhul-Qarnayn.[1] He was traveling one day and reached a place where the sun was setting in a muddy spring. The text didn't say that it was setting *behind* a muddy spring, nor did it say it *appeared* to be setting in a muddy spring. According to the hadith, the sun itself had reduced to a minute fraction of its actual size and heat, entered the earth's atmosphere, and landed in a puddle. This struck me as ridiculous. How could the book of Allah have something so scientifically wrong in it?

I continued my search in the Qur'an, hoping to remind myself what it taught about the history of Allah's people. Like most Muslims, I had been encouraged to read a few verses here and there, jumping from place to place without ever starting from the beginning and reading all the way through. We relied on the mullah to explain the words for us, and we were not encouraged to read more than a few verses for ourselves.

I decided to see what the Qur'an had to say about Abraham and Joseph, two men whose stories I had loved hearing about from the mullahs when I was growing up. I discovered that Abraham's story was only partially told, the verses scattered like petals in a hurricane. There was no logic to it, no coherent structure for me to follow.

At least Joseph's story was all in one place. The problem was that there was so little to it. The Qur'an starts by explaining that Joseph was so beautiful that when he walked by some women peeling potatoes, they stared at him and accidentally cut their hands. Then I read that Potiphar's wife wanted to marry Joseph, but he refused because he was Allah's faithful servant. I was curious to find out what happened to him next, but the story ends abruptly there.[2]

Jonah's story is scattered like Abraham's. The Qur'an says he was a messenger and talks about the whale and Jonah's message to the people of Nineveh. But in various places, Jonah is described as being in the belly of the whale for one, three, seven, or forty days.

I started to wonder who wrote the Qur'an. I knew it wasn't Hazrat Muhammad, because he was illiterate. From what I could tell, after Muhammad's death, as his successors battled for control, people were invited to submit any stories they remembered about the Prophet. Some wrote on goatskins; some wrote on stones. In all, seven copies of the Qur'an were created. Then at some point, six of the copies were burned, leaving just one behind.

I wondered why.

†

Testing the trustworthiness of the Qur'an was a slow process. It is not an easy book to read, even in translation, and for weeks I tried to decode the pages, following the narrative as it jumped from place to place. Gradually the text came into sharper focus, and as it did, I found myself looking at Muhammad in a new light.

I had never questioned him before. I'd never doubted him. I'd never had any cause to think of him as anything other than the last and greatest Prophet. Never in my life had I uttered his name without adding the words "peace be upon him."

But now I started to wonder about Muhammad himself. Stories that had delighted me as a child suddenly left an unpleasant aftertaste. So when I read about him fighting and taking prisoners, I no longer rejoiced in his power; I recoiled at his cruelty. I felt even worse when I read how one of those prisoners was a beautiful girl. She was taken to Muhammad, who said that if she married him, he would set her free. "It's good for me to die in prison rather than be your wife," she said. She was sent back to jail, where she died.

There's also a story about an old widow who approached Muhammad and asked if Muhammad would marry her. Writing in the hadith, the narrator describes the way Muhammad looked at her from head to toe, saw she was old and not beautiful, and said to his followers, "Whoever will marry this person will go to heaven." One man agreed but explained that he had no money to give her for a dowry. "Do you have a shawl?" Muhammad asked. "Give that to her." The man did, and the two were married.

It struck me as wrong that the Prophet would be so influenced by physical beauty. Surely for a prophet of Allah, it should not matter one bit whether someone is old or young, beautiful or ugly. Shouldn't Allah's messengers dispense his mercy freely?

I could not deny everything about Muhammad. I still appreciated some of the stories, like the one where a non-Muslim woman dumped her trash on him every day. One day she became sick and couldn't leave the house, so Muhammad visited her. Instead of seeking revenge, he gave her water and medicine. She became a Muslim soon after.

This was the Muhammad I had been brought up to follow.

How could I feel the same loyalty when I read about the time when he saw a blind man and turned his face away from him?[3] Why would he withhold mercy from someone whose affliction wasn't his own fault?

The struggle within me grew fiercer. At times I felt as though I were going mad. Nothing made sense like it used to.

To my parents, I appeared to be diligent and devoted, the perfect daughter who was preparing to make the perfect sacrifice. When I wasn't at college, I spent nearly all my time in the prayer room or on the roof, with the Qur'an open on my lap.

But appearances can be deceptive. Inside, I was starting to fear that my previously strong faith in Islam might not last much longer. To the outside world, I was pouring the words of the Qur'an into my soul. Internally, I was beginning to question whether any of the words I read could be trusted.

Every week I called the hospital. I figured that if anyone found out, they would assume I was checking on my mother's treatment. In truth, I was speaking to John.

Every time we spoke, he'd ask me what I had been reading. "What do you think? Is it true? Are you finding the answers to your questions yet?"

"No," I said more than once. "Just more questions."

†

My mother had taught me well. From my earliest days, long before I attended the madrassa, I'd been able to recite my five daily prayers. I'd also known all the key scriptures that helped to outline exactly what it meant to be a Muslim:

O you who have believed, believe in Allah and His
Messenger and the Book that He sent down upon
His Messenger and the Scripture which He sent down
before. And whoever disbelieves in Allah, His angels,
His books, His messengers, and the Last Day has
certainly gone far astray.[4]

I knew the hadith as well:

One day while Allah's Apostle was sitting with
the people, a man came to him walking and said,
"O Allah's Apostle. What is Belief?" The Prophet
said, "Belief is to believe in Allah, His Angels, His
Books, His Apostles, and the meeting with Him,
and to believe in the Resurrection."[5]

The same message is found in another hadith:

Abu Huraira reported: One day the Messenger of
Allah (may peace be upon him) appeared before the
public that a man came to him and said: Prophet of
Allah, (tell me) what is Iman. Upon this he (the Holy
Prophet) replied: That you affirm your faith in Allah,
His angels, His Books, His meeting, His Messengers
and that you affirm your faith in the Resurrection
hereafter."[6]

Every one of those passages mentions "books." None of
them refer to a singular book, as if only the Qur'an is to be followed. *Books* doesn't point to just the hadith, either. This term
refers to four different books: the Torah (the first five books
of the Old Testament, as revealed to Moses), the Zabur (or

the Psalms, as revealed to David), the Injil (or the Gospel, as revealed to Jesus), and the Qur'an (as revealed to Muhammad). In other words, to be a good Muslim, you have to believe in the Bible.

Having struggled to find the truth in the Qur'an, it was only a matter of time before I told my mother I was feeling ill and needed to make an appointment to visit the hospital and have some blood tests conducted myself.

The next day I was standing in front of John's desk. "Please," I begged, "give me your Holy Bible. I know it contains three of the books all Muslims should read."

"I'm so sorry, but I can't give it to you. Do you know what happens to Christians around here if they get caught handing out Bibles to Muslims?"

I told him I didn't, and he recounted stories about churches being burned to the ground, Christians being charged with blasphemy and sentenced to death, and clerics offering vast rewards to people who hunted down Christians accused of handing out Bibles. "If I gave you a Bible, they would use it as an excuse to persecute even more Christians in this city."

I listened in silence, struggling to take it all in. I wanted to doubt every word he said, to discount it as lies and propaganda, but I knew I could not. Based on my field trips with the madrassa and the way my mother reacted when my father did business with a Christian, I knew he was telling the truth. Pakistan was a dangerous place for Christians.

All at once I was struck by the risk John was taking just by talking to me. He'd lose more than his job if he was caught. He would more than likely pay with his life. And if he had a family, they would be lucky to escape unscathed. At best, they would be thrown out of their home and forced to leave the city. At worst, their deaths would become part of somebody's jihad.

What would he say if he knew about my plans for jihad? How would he treat me if he realized I was one of those Muslims for whom killing Christians like him is an act of duty? I couldn't imagine that he would be willing to be in the same room as me, let alone treat me with such warmth and kindness.

A silence settled between us. Normally I would have taken it as my sign that the conversation was over and that I was being dismissed. I would lower my eyes and leave. But John was not like any other man I had met. Though we barely knew each other, in his eyes I saw nothing but trust and acceptance.

"Whenever you want to read the Holy Bible," he said gently, "you can come here and read it. It's always quiet in the afternoon, and I'd be happy to let you read it."

I wanted so much to tell him the truth about me. And I wanted so much to hide my past.

When I spoke next, my voice was quiet.

"Aren't you scared I'll tell people about you?"

He looked straight at me. Such trust. Such acceptance. "No." There was no hesitation in his voice, no doubt in his eyes. He held my stare for a moment, then broke it when someone appeared at the door and asked him a question about some results they were waiting for.

I stepped back and waited for the door to close.

When we were alone again, I told him I needed to get home and would return in a few days. I turned to leave, but something held me back. I looked at him and spoke the words I had been fearing for months: "I don't think I'm a Muslim anymore."

"Wow," he said, wearing the widest smile I had ever seen. "That's really good."

"Is it?" I said. I wasn't so sure. But I hoped he was right.

13

My mother believed me when I told her that I was starting a new practicum at college and would therefore need to stay after class every day for a couple of hours. If I'd done my calculations correctly, that would allow me enough time to walk to the hospital, spend an hour reading with John, and be back on the steps of the college when my brother arrived to pick me up.

When I showed up at John's lab at the agreed-upon time the following week, he led me to a cluttered desk in the corner. I sat with my back to the wall, the desktop hidden from view by an old computer screen, and watched as he took a book out of his bag and placed it in front of me.

"This is it?"

"The Holy Bible," he said.

I stared at it. It had a black cover, just as Anwar had told me, but it was half the size of the Qur'an. I was surprised by how nervous I felt.

"It's okay—you can open it," John said as he returned to his desk on the other side of the room.

I continued to stare at the book. For years when I was learning to read the Qur'an, I did so only with a cleric at my side. The mullah would select the passages he wanted me to read, turn the pages, and lead my study. It was only when I got to the madrassa that I started to read the Qur'an on my own.

"But where do I start?" I called out.

John returned and showed me the book of Genesis. "You start at the beginning."

†

I looked up to find John standing over me. "Don't you need to go now?" he said, looking at the clock. Almost an hour had passed, but it had felt like mere moments. I said good-bye and told him I would see him tomorrow. Then I stumbled into the evening crowds and hurried back to the college.

My head was alive, and everything I had read in that hour was stirring and sparking within me. To my surprise, I understood it all. The stories in Genesis answered questions I didn't even know I was asking. The book showed why there are seven days in a week and why people throughout the world take at least one day off to rest. It explained the sin that Adam and Eve committed and the reason Abraham's sons fought and divided.

The next day I barely said a word to John as I hurried to the desk. I was like a prisoner set free. The more of this freedom I tasted, the more I wanted.

As soon as I read the story of Joseph, I closed the book and sat back, lost in thought.

"What is it?" John asked.

"The dream that Joseph had—it reminds me of a dream I had." I let my mind return to the graveyard and the light and the golden walls and the ocean-like crystal floor. "If I share it with you, can you interpret it for me?"

"I'm not sure, but I'll do my best."

When I finished, John had tears in his eyes, along with the same wide smile I'd seen the week before.

"What is it?"

"Praise God," he whispered. "You are in God's plan. He has chosen you."

"What do you mean?"

He picked up the Bible, turned to a new page, and handed it back to me. "Read this," he said, his finger pointing to a verse.

I did as he said, and my voice filled the room. "Jesus answered, 'I am the way and the truth and the life. No one comes to the Father except through me.'"[7]

I looked at the page again. I read the verse aloud once more. I looked back at John, whose tears were flowing freely now.

"You are honored that Jesus Christ, the Lord of lords and the King of kings, appeared to you himself."

Then it was my turn to cry. My tears felt warm as they fell down my cheeks. I tried to wipe them away, but it was no use. There were too many to stop.

"Why?" I asked. "Why these words when there are so many others in the Bible?"

"The first time we met, do you remember what you said to me?"

I shrugged. I remembered everything from that day, but I was having trouble finding the words.

"You told me that Islam is the only true way. I knew then that you were a faithful Muslim, that you were following diligently and honestly. You didn't know that Islam is not the way of eternal life, that it is spiritually dead and covered in darkness. In your dream, you were among the dead, trapped in the graveyard. But you were looking for a way out—you were willing to leave the graveyard. My Lord Jesus Christ is well acquainted with all our spiritual needs, and your needs were no different. You needed to know the truth, and you needed to know the way out. That's why he said, 'I am the way, the truth, and the life'—because those were the most important words you needed to hear."

"But why did he call me Esther? Surely he knew what my name is."

John took the Bible again, found what he was looking for, and handed it back to me. When I'd finished reading, I had nothing to say. I could barely lift my head as John spoke.

"He called you Esther so you would know that he has chosen you. He found you here, in the middle of millions of Muslims. He knows you. He has a plan for you. He has called you for such a time as this."

Ever since I'd sat in the lab the previous day, a strange sensation had been growing in me. At first I thought I was just tired, but as it became stronger, I realized it was not fatigue but heaviness. There was a weight resting within me. It was as if gravity had shifted, as if some new planet had caught me in its pull. As I listened to John speak, the feeling made sense: I no longer belonged to the world as I knew it. I belonged somewhere else.

"Please," I said, "what do I have to do to be a Christian?"

"Is that what you want?"

"Yes," I said. "I do."

He exhaled and checked the room again, even though we'd been alone since I arrived. "First of all, you have to say the sinner's prayer. Later, you will need to be baptized, but I'll explain about that in time. Every day you pray and read the Holy Bible. Do all those, and you will be a Christian."

"I want to start now. Teach me the prayer."

I listened carefully to what he said, repeating each phrase exactly. Some of the phrases were new to me—"died on the cross," "purchased by your holy sacrifice," "you are alive and always with us"—but that did nothing to quench the new pulsing in my veins. I was alive.

†

From that day on, John no longer called me Zakhira. I wanted him to call me Esther, the name Jesus himself had given me. Every day after class, I returned to his lab, hungry to devour more of the precious Holy Bible.

My mind was full of questions about the words I read. I got stuck many times, but at every point, John was there to help.

"How can the Bible say there is one God when there are clearly three?"

"Think of an egg," John said. "You have the white, the yolk, and the shell. They're all different, but together they make up one single thing. God is unified just the same. Or think of this: What is the chemical formula for ice?"

"H_2O."

"Okay. And what is the chemical formula for water?"

"H_2O," I said again.

"Good. And what about steam?"

"It's the same."

"Exactly. They're all different expressions of the same thing. That's like the Trinity. God chose to show himself in three different ways—Father, Son, and Holy Spirit—but they are all the same God."

John also taught me how Christians pray and worship. He explained what happens when they meet together in church and how baptism marks the point at which a Christian is formally welcomed into the church.

As soon as he explained baptism, my mind was made up. "I want to go to church with you, and I want to have baptism," I said.

"You mean you want to get baptized," John corrected gently. "And you will. In time I will take you to church, you will meet my pastor, and he will baptize you. But it would not be safe to do it now—not for you or for the church. So you need to wait, study the Bible, and pray."

I'll admit that I found it all a little frustrating. Having left Islam behind, I wanted to belong to Christianity. Even though I had decided in my heart that I was going to follow Jesus, I felt homeless. I was desperate for anything that would help me put down new roots.

When I asked John for the twentieth time to give me a Bible of my own, he replied with the same smile and polite refusal that he had given me nineteen times before. As I left the lab and made the familiar walk home, I felt disappointment lodging inside me. When would I be able to officially be part of God's family?

†

Nobody except John knew about my conversion to Christianity, but he and I had no contact outside his lab. So apart from one hour every weekday, I was alone, living the life of a secret believer.

It was a condition that was entirely new to me. Even though I'd been accustomed to sharing virtually none of my life with my father, my mother and I had always been close. Until I became a Christian, I had no secrets from her at all. With my heart now closed to Islam and my thoughts fixed on Jesus, everything within me had shifted dramatically. Yet whenever possible, I had to keep up appearances of being a good Muslim. If anyone found out the truth about my new-found faith, I would be as good as dead.

Whenever I was in public, I continued wearing the same Islamic veil I'd been wearing since I joined the madrassa. At home I still gathered with my family in the prayer room as we rolled out our mats. Only when they held their hands to their ears and cried out with loud voices, "Allahu Akbar!" I said softly, "Hal-le-lu-jah!" When they crossed their hands over their chests, knelt down, and put their hands on their knees before touching their foreheads to the ground, I did so too, but my heart and mind were fixed on Jesus.

I had committed a number of psalms to memory—Psalms 16, 20, 23, 34, 91, 121, and 123—and they helped me greatly. I recited them so often that their words flowed like a silent stream within me. "You make known to me the path of life . . ." At any point I could step back from life in my Muslim household, with its rules and judgments about what constituted a good servant of Islam, and retreat into my mind. "The LORD is my shepherd . . ." There I found love, mercy, honest repentance, and the assurance of forgiveness. Islam had taught me to fear Allah, to never forget the prospect of eternal judgment and the brutal torture of hell. The psalms reminded me of the love of God—a love so great it overcomes all fear and death. A love that was mine, even though I could never do enough to deserve it. "The LORD will watch over your coming and going both now and forevermore . . ."

I did allow myself one small change to my outward behavior after becoming Christian. All my life, whenever I'd spoken or written the name Muhammad, I'd always followed it with the words "peace be upon him," just as I had been taught. Somehow that felt wrong now. So I started adding the word *hazrat*—an honorific reserved for leaders and high officials—when I said Muhammad's name. Everybody who heard it assumed I was using the word as a sign of respect, but I preferred the word's other meaning: scheming.

†

John knew that the consequence of trying to convert a Muslim to Christianity was death, so he continued to deny my requests for a Bible. That's why I was surprised when one day he gave me an audiocassette of some Christians singing worship songs to God in Punjabi. I brought it home, went up to my bedroom, and played Psalm 103. "Bless the Lord, O my soul," proclaimed the song. I closed my eyes and let the music soothe me.

"Zakhira, what is this music?" My mother was standing in the doorway, looking puzzled.

"It is a song that praises Allah," I spluttered, my heart racing.

"I haven't heard it before. Is it naat?" she asked. The only songs my mother ever sang or played in the house were traditional songs that praised Muhammad.

"No, it's not naat. These songs are only about Allah."

She stood and listened for a while. I was desperate for her to leave, and I prayed that God would give me the words to say if she didn't.

"Where did you get it?"

"A friend at college gave it to me. She said that one of the mullahs gave it to her and that everyone should hear it and sing along. They want people to learn how to praise Allah, who is our creator, not just Hazrat Muhammad. They say your house will prosper if you do." I felt bad lying to her, but I could not risk telling her the truth.

She stood in silence for a while, the song continuing to

declare the goodness of God. "I like it," she said, before turning to leave.

She liked it so much that later she asked me to bring the cassette downstairs. Every morning she played the songs and sang along. She even gave the cassette to her friends to listen to, telling them they needed to get their own copies as well.

I loved hearing the house fill with the sounds of my mother singing along: "The steadfast love of the Lord is from everlasting to everlasting on those who fear him." It made me smile to listen, and I knew the words were true. God's love really was enough; it really was unbreakable, eternal, everlasting.

I was so happy I almost gave up on pestering John to give me a Bible.

Almost, but not quite.

14

"Esther, you know I wish I could give you a copy of the Holy Bible, but I can't," John said when I asked for the last time. "If someone found out . . . But remember this—God knows all our needs. In his perfect timing and in his perfect way, he always responds."

Several months had passed since I had my dream. Not having a Bible at home meant I continued to read the Qur'an. What I read did nothing to change my mind about Islam—in fact, it only presented me with more evidence against the faith. It also gave my mother the impression that I was still a devout Muslim. Perhaps that is why she never brought up the subject of my going to jihad training. And since nobody from the training camp called to check on me, the subject seemed to fade into the background.

One afternoon, as my brother drove into the courtyard

after picking me up from college, I noticed that something unusual was happening a little farther down the street. A group of women was standing outside the home of one of our neighbors, and people were shouting at them from across the street. Of the six women, three were clearly Westerners, and three looked like they were from Southeast Asia.

My brother noticed me looking at them. "Christians," he said. "They've been in the neighborhood all day. I'm amazed they're still here."

We hurried into the house. I'd told God so many times that I didn't think it would be difficult for him to give me a Bible. I knew without a doubt that these women were his way of showing me that he had heard my pleas for help.

My mother and sister were watching from inside, looking at the women with a combination of intrigue and mild disgust.

"Have they been here yet?" I asked.

"No. But if they come, I'll send them away without even opening the door."

"But why?" I asked. "If they're Christians, wouldn't it be better for us to let them in? Isn't that what Hazrat Muhammad would do? Think of the story of the old woman who threw trash on him every day. Instead of pushing them out, let's do something nice. Maybe then they'll come to Islam."

Soon after, when they knocked on our door, my mother could not have been more polite. She smiled warmly, showed them into the drawing room, made sure they were comfortable, and offered them food and drink. Their Urdu was limited, and my mother's English was nonexistent, but I kept quiet, wanting to observe them for a while. They mimed that they were not hungry, but my mother had my sister bring in a bowl of oranges that were so fresh that soon the whole room was filled with their scent.

"Now," my mother said once we were all settled, "would you like to become Muslims? It doesn't take long—just a quick trip to the mosque, where you can say a *kalma* to confess faith in Allah, and you'll be done. What do you think?"

The six women shifted uncomfortably but said nothing in reply. As my mother, sister, and brother talked among themselves about whether the women had understood or not, I leaned over and spoke quietly with one of the Western women.

"Nobody in my family can understand English, but I do. And nobody knows I'm a Christian."

Her eyes widened in amazement. She looked at me deeply for a moment, a trace of concern flickering across her face before smiling broadly. "Wow, I'm so glad."

"Nobody knows—please don't tell," I said. "But I was so moved when I saw you out on the street, getting treated badly like that. That really encouraged me. It reminded me of what happened to the first apostles."

I looked at my mother, who was trying to engage the other five women in a discussion about Muhammad. Nobody on either side seemed to understand what was being said.

"I need a Bible," I said quietly. "I've been trying to get one for months, but I haven't been able to. Can you help me?"

She shook her head. "I can't, but I know someone you can write to who might be able to help." Checking to make sure no one was watching, she reached into her bag, pulled out a business card, and passed it to me.

My mother, frustrated at her failure to convert our guests, ushered them out of the house. I hung back in the room and inspected the card. *Pakistan Bible Society.* If they couldn't help, I figured nobody could.

†

The next day, the lectures on campus had all been canceled. I'd deliberately not told anyone about it. After my brother dropped me off at the courtyard, I called John from a phone booth. There was no reply at the lab, so I tried his home.

I had obviously woken him up, and he did not sound as pleased to hear from me as I'd hoped.

"I have a whole day free. Can I spend it reading at the lab?"

"I'm sorry," he said. "It's my one day off, and I'm planning to spend it resting."

"Fine!" I spat, grinding down the receiver. I didn't need him anyway. I could find my own Bible.

I pulled out the card and looked at the address I had already memorized. It was in the city, but the PO box gave me no clue as to where. I thought about going to the post office and seeing if I could find a street address, but the idea was unlikely to succeed—and very risky.

Instead, I opted for plan C. I headed to the post office, bought a sheet of paper, and sat along a quiet side street writing a letter.

I believe in Jesus Christ, but I need a Bible to read.
Please send one to me.

I decided to include my home address but not my name. Then I considered my next problem. To send a letter in Pakistan, you have to pay for postage at the post office, where they fill out the address details on the envelope. Telling a clerk that I wanted to write to the Pakistan Bible Society would raise suspicions. So I folded the letter into a shape that looked like an envelope, addressed it myself, adding my return address on the back, and posted it in the box out front. I hoped it would reach them even though it didn't have a stamp—and that I would be able to intercept the Bible before anyone else at home opened it.

What I didn't factor in was that my homemade envelope, the lack of a stamp, and the addressee made my letter highly visible. It never made it to the Bible Society. Instead, it was opened up by a curious postal worker, who passed it on to my neighborhood postman. He paid my uncle a visit, asking him what connection he had with Christians.

"I don't know any of them," my uncle said.

"But someone in your sister's house does."

My uncle opened the letter and read it.

By the time he made it to my house, he was sure he knew who had written it.

"I recognize your handwriting," he said to me as he stood in the doorway.

"Yes," I said. "It's mine."

"Where's your father?"

"He's out. Nobody else is at home—just me."

He left without saying a word. I didn't know what to do—I spent the next hour alternating between doing chores around the house and looking out the window, wondering how long it would be before my uncle returned. I could not settle down. My muscles and my brain were too wired to stick to any task for more than a few minutes.

When my parents returned, I waited anxiously for them to ask about the letter. I stayed in the kitchen for a while, but no such conversation took place. My mother and father acted as if everything was normal.

I went upstairs and did what I wished I had done as soon as my uncle left. I knelt down and prayed. "Lord, you are my

Good Shepherd . . ." As soon as I said those words, I knew I was not alone.

†

My sense of peace was shattered later that evening. It was dark outside when I heard a crowd of people gathering in the street. I recognized a few of them—mainly members of my family and regulars from the daras—but many of the one-hundred-strong crowd were strangers to me. And nearly all of them were holding a single piece of paper.

My mother burst into my room, her hand clenched around the same photocopy the people on the street were holding. I did not need to look at it to know what it was.

"What's this letter about?"

In that moment, the breath leaked out of me. I felt utterly isolated. Cold. Alone. My secret was out.

I tried to find the words to pray. *Hallelujah,* I said inside. *Only you can save me.* But it was not a prayer of victory or a statement of confidence. It was a plea of fearful desperation. My fear was not just for myself but for my parents. I worried that they would get in trouble, that they would be scolded by our community.

"Why did you write this letter?"

My mother was angry, and as I looked at her, the slightest change happened within me. I found a kernel of courage inside—so small it was barely noticeable. But as I listened to myself reply, I was surprised by what I said and how calmly I said it. "I just want to see what's in the Christians' book. Don't we say all the time, 'I believe in Allah. I believe that the angels exist. I believe in the four books from Allah, his prophets, and the judgment day'? We say this every day, so why not read the book that contains the Torah, the Zabur, and the Injil?"

My mother stared at me, silent.

"Come outside," she finally said.

They made me sit on the ground in the middle of the crowd, opposite a mullah who was also seated on the ground. Throngs of men and women towered above me, their hatred palpable. The mullah asked the same question my mother had asked, and I gave the same answer: "If we say we believe in the four books from Allah, what makes the Bible so bad?"

"We don't need the Bible!" someone shouted.

"I just wanted to read it," I said to the mullah.

"Yes," he said, "but you claimed to believe in Jesus. Are you a Christian now?"

Before I could answer, the crowd surged forward.

"She's under blasphemy! She must die!"

"Burn her!"

"Shoot her!"

The mullah waved them away. "There must be some reason why you did it."

"I just wrote because I want to see . . ."

"No!" my uncle said to the crowd. "It was the women who came to visit their house. There were some white women among them. They made her do it! It's their fault."

"*Kafir*! Infidel!"

The mullah stared at me. The shouting continued, growing louder with each question I answered. Even if I'd had something to say in that moment, I doubt I would have been heard.

I let my thoughts drift. Would they string me up by a rope and hang me from a streetlamp? *Everyone has to die sometime.* What could I do?

It seemed like ages passed before the mullah spoke again. "Let's think carefully about this," he said. "We all know that this girl is a strong believer in Islam, and we've all seen the good work she does among the poor. We should take her to the mufti and see what he says."

†

We walked to the mosque in a giant crowd. I wasn't sure how many people followed the mullah, my father, his friends, and me, but it felt like we filled the whole street as we walked. I was in the front, with my father's strong hands clasped around my arms.

As we passed in front of shops with brightly lit signs and curious men watching from plastic tables and chairs, I prayed silently. *O Lord Jesus, you are my refuge and strength. You are my ever-present help in times of trouble. I commit the judge they're taking me to into your mighty and miraculous hands. Lord Jesus, please take his mind under your control. I pour your precious and holy blood over him from head to toe. You shed your blood for sinners like me. Whatever the judge decides, may it come from you. I just want you to be exalted and glorified. If you're willing that I should come to you today, Lord Jesus, I'm ready. Whatever your will is for me, let it be done tonight.*

By the time we arrived at the mosque, I was reciting psalms in my head. Even so, however, there was a struggle within me. I trusted God, and the thought of death itself did not scare me, but I worried that my death would cause pain and trouble for my parents.

Then, for the first time in my life, I heard a gentle, divine whisper in my ear. *I have called you by name. I will go before you and level the mountains. All who rage against you will surely be ashamed and disgraced. And you will know that I am the Lord your God.*

"Amen," I said out loud. Confidence surged within me as we walked into the mosque. "Amen."

†

The room I was taken to was deep inside the mosque. There were no windows—just three doors and a bunch of thin mattresses along the wall to sit on. I was directed to sit by myself on one of the mattresses, while the others—my parents, my uncle, and a handful of other people from the crowd—sat on the other mattresses. I kept my eyes on the dark red carpet at my feet, aware that if I looked up, I'd see them all staring at me.

I had no fear swelling in me, no panic. The words of my Lord were all I needed. I trusted my faithful God—the one who is true to all his promises.

As soon as I sat down, the mullah and several other older men from the crowd disappeared. When I looked up, I saw that they had returned with two new men. The first, I assumed, was the mufti, the judge. He was a large man, older than my father. His white hair and full beard circled his head like a cloud.

The second was Anwar.

I had not seen him for more than a year. When I started college, I stopped meeting with him for tutorials, and even though he was still the head of the militants in the city, he and I had never spoken about my decision to say yes to jihad.

In many ways, I'd missed him. He was the one who persuaded my father to let me remain in school. He was the one who nurtured my love of science. And he was the one who suggested that the Bible could answer some of my questions about Islam.

But I feared him too.

As I sat on the mattress and looked at him, he gave me the same stare as when I had asked him about time travel or the fate of the dinosaurs. His eyes locked on mine, examining me.

The mufti was holding a copy of my letter in his hand, as well as a few books of hadith.

He cleared his throat. "I haven't found anything that declares that she is an apostate or that she is a Christian or that she is blasphemous. In this letter, she didn't write anything against the Qur'an; anything against our prophet Muhammad, peace be upon him; or anything against Islam. She wrote in her letter that she believes in the prophet Jesus, and she asked for a Bible. This is one of the five core beliefs: faith in one Allah, faith in the angels of Allah, faith in the four books (Torah, Zabur, Injil, and Qur'an), faith in the prophets of Allah, and faith in the day of judgment.

"As Muslims, we can't deny the prophet Jesus, because he's a great prophet among all the prophets from Allah. We must believe in him. If we deny any one of these conditions of faith, we are not Muslim."

He turned to me as he went on. "You asked for a Holy Bible. Why? Do you know that these books have been changed?"

"Anwar told me to," I said, summoning up as much volume and confidence as I could manage. The room fell silent. I could feel Anwar's eyes on me. I kept my gaze on the judge. "I once told him that I wanted to know about all the prophets and their teachings in great detail and asked which book I should read to find out more. He told me there is only one book with that kind of information—the Bible. I asked where I could get the book, and he told me I could only get it from Christians. He said it was better that I didn't approach Christians but that he would find a copy and give it to me. After waiting for some time, when he didn't give me the Holy Bible, I wrote this letter."

The judge paused and then turned to look at Anwar.

"Yes," Anwar said. "She did ask me this once, and I replied as she has said."

Silence filled the room again. I looked around me. Nobody caught my eye except Anwar. His stare was the same as before.

"Anwar is correct," the judge eventually said. "It's good that you want to know more about the prophets and that you want to increase your knowledge. But first you need to be mature and strong in Qur'an and Islam. Only then can you read that book."

"Very well," I said, feeling as bold as I had ever felt in my life. "I'll wait until I'm ready."

Turning to the others in the room, the judge continued. "There's no reason to kill her, for she isn't under blasphemy. If she'd said she was a Christian, that would bring death upon her. But she didn't, and I believe she has a good heart. She is eager to learn. Her mullah and Anwar have told me that she is very punctual in offering all her prayers. I'd like to say that she is better than all of you."

To my father, he said, "Be careful, though. She is a little bit interested in these things. Keep an eye on her, and don't let it go any further. Give her more Islamic books to read. Treat her kindly."

If the walk to the mosque had felt like a funeral march, the walk home was a wedding party. People were cheering and laughing, apologizing to me and praising me for the ways I had impressed the mufti. They bought me sweets and sodas and stood outside my house threatening to wake the whole city with their celebrations. Everyone appeared to be as relieved as I was.

Everyone, that is, except my father. From the moment the mufti had delivered his final warning, my father's jaw had clenched and his eyes turned away. He kept his distance from me as we walked home, and I could not be sure why. Was he relieved and repentant, or did he still doubt my story?

It was all too much. As soon as I could, I left the cheering crowd in the street outside, ran straight to my room, and collapsed into bed.

15

Even though I was convinced of the power of God's mighty hand, I decided I needed to be more careful. No more trying to get a Bible from strangers, no more taking risks that could put Christians in danger. And no more contact with John.

Not seeing John was the hardest decision of all. Those afternoons spent in his lab reading and talking about the Bible were always the highlight of my day, and I dreaded the hole that would be left behind when I didn't see him anymore. For months he had been my guide, my teacher, and my friend. He had challenged me, surprised me, and on more than one occasion, driven me mad. He was patient, kind, and brave. Most of all, he had shown me what it means to truly love God and others.

I arranged one final meeting at the lab. As soon as I arrived, I told John what had happened and shown him the fatwa the mufti had given to my parents after my hearing. The decree made it clear that I was innocent of the charge of blasphemy, but there was a line toward the end that John's eyes kept returning to: *She did not write that she was a Christian. If she had, it would be right to kill her.*

John looked at me. I offered him a weak smile, but his face remained fixed. He reached for his Bible and asked me to read from Matthew 10:22: "You will be hated by everyone because of me, but the one who stands firm to the end will be saved."

When I finished reading, he took the Bible back from me. "It will happen just as Jesus said. Your future may be more difficult than anything you've faced yet. Are you still willing to follow him?"

I didn't need any time to consider my reply. "Jesus is like oxygen for me," I said. "You know that no one can live without oxygen, don't you? So how can I live without him?"

At last John smiled. "Praise God," he said. "Hallelujah."

"I can't come here again, though. It's too dangerous for you, and for your church, too. I don't want to cause trouble for any of you."

"I know," he said. "You're right. We shouldn't see each other again." I was surprised how sad he sounded.

Then he prayed for me, asking God to grant me protection and wisdom, and for the power of the Holy Spirit to lead me and guide me.

"Amen," I said. When I opened my eyes, I saw that he was holding his Bible in front of him.

"Take it," he said. "It's yours."

†

Every step of my journey home, I was aware of the precious treasure I was carrying in my bag. When I was in my room, I took it out and held it tight. The familiar shape and smell of the book I had handled almost every day for months suddenly felt mysterious and dangerous in this new environment. I hid it in my closet and brought it out again only when I was sure everyone in my family was asleep.

As difficult as it was to quit the habit of visiting John after classes, I quickly adopted a new routine of going to bed early, then waking up when the house was dark and silent to read the Bible. Sometimes I would spend minutes kissing and hugging the book before I started reading. It was the light of my eyes and the peace of my heart.

I never felt bored when I read the Bible, and I followed the program John had given me: first a chapter from the Old Testament, followed by one from the Psalms or Proverbs, then a chapter from the New Testament. I repeated the cycle countless times each day, and within three months, I had finished reading the whole book. So I started again.

Everything I read fascinated me, and with each chapter, I could feel my faith growing. I loved the way the book of Proverbs showed me exactly how life was supposed to be lived, while the Gospel of John, the book of Acts, and Revelation filled my head with such vivid images and scenes that I felt as though I were right there watching the events unfold. Reading about the persecution of Christians encouraged me greatly, especially the account of Stephen. For days I thought about what a privilege it would be to die as a martyr.

The book of Job inspired me too. Even though he'd done nothing wrong, God tested him. I liked the idea that we can't just take the good from God. We have to accept hard times too. Will we turn away when trials come, or will we bow before God, trusting him in the midst of our troubles?

One night, after reading about Peter climbing out of the boat and panicking, I had a dream that was just as real as the one I'd had in the prayer room. I was in a boat, surrounded by an ocean so vast that I couldn't see the shore in any direction. As I looked, a storm struck up in the distance. It was raging with all the ferocity of hell, and I knew the water was going to drown me and claim me for its own. The waves were approaching fast, and it would not be long before they reached me. In my dream, I did the only thing I knew to do: I closed my eyes and declared my trust in God. "Okay," I said, putting my foot out of the boat. I felt the water whipping and slashing at my ankle. "I trust you."

The minute my foot touched the surface of the water, I felt something unexpected beneath me. A rock. I swung my other leg from the boat and placed that one down too. Again, I brought my foot down on solid ground. I took another step forward, then another, and another. Though the storm continued to rage around me, my path was secure. I knew that if I trusted God, things were going to work out just the way he wanted them to.

†

One of my engineering requirements for college included taking an extended placement with a local business. I was happy enough for the opportunity, though not because I cared about the task I'd been assigned—conducting market research for a food company—but because I hoped it might offer me a little more time to read my Bible.

I was right.

On the first day, during my lunch break, I found a quiet corner, pulled out my lunch, and started reading.

"What are you reading?"

I looked up and saw the supervisor standing over me. He had introduced himself to me and the other students earlier in the day, and he'd made us laugh with his jokes about chicken cubes and how terrible he was at cooking.

I looked at him and decided this was worth the risk. "The Holy Bible."

He looked confused. "What's it about?"

"I'm a Christian, and this is all about the prophets."

"But you have a Muslim name."

"My parents just liked Zakhira, that's all."

He thought for a while. "You should become a Muslim. Have you read the Qur'an?"

"Yes."

"Oh. Why?"

"Because I wanted to understand it. I studied it and found that there are so many inconsistencies in it. I even highlighted a bunch of them."

"You highlighted the Qur'an? Really?"

"Yes."

For the first time in our conversation, he smiled. "Can you bring it in? I would be fascinated to see it."

"Yes!" I said, encouraged. "I will bring it for you tomorrow."

As promised, I took the Qur'an in the next day. I tried to read my supervisor's face as he flicked through the pages striped with yellow, orange, blue, and pink lines, but he gave nothing away.

"I'm a science student," I added, wondering if he needed a little encouragement to admit that he was skeptical too. "I can't believe that Allah would write this."

"Oh," he said. "This is very interesting. Can I borrow it?"

"Of course!"

I prayed hard for the man that night. This was my first attempt at evangelizing someone, and so far, it had been a lot easier than I'd thought it would be. I'd sown the seeds of doubt, and surely it would not be long before he saw Islam for what it was.

†

The next day I noticed that the rest of my fellow students weren't going inside as usual. "There's a problem," one girl said to me. "We've been told to wait."

Soon after, my supervisor came out. "Everybody should leave and come back tomorrow," he said. "Except for you, Zakhira. You need to follow me inside. The boss wants to see you."

He took me upstairs and showed me into an office dominated by a large desk, my copy of the Qur'an the sole object upon it. I had never seen the boss before, but even from behind the desk, he was an intimidating presence. He dismissed my supervisor as soon as I was inside. Without taking his eyes off me, he picked up my copy of the Qur'an.

"Zakhira, is this yours?"

I could feel my insides twisting. "Yes."

"Did you highlight it? Are these your marks inside?"

"Yes."

"Do you have all your belongings with you?" he asked quietly.

"Yes."

"I studied in a school run by Christian missionaries. You need to run out the back door. I won't open the main door until you're far away. Do you have enough money for a rickshaw home?"

I shook my head, and he handed me some cash along with my Qur'an.

A smile settled on his face. "I know that Christians are good people. And I know that God will protect you. Now go."

✝

Back at college, nobody was interested in why I had been sent away from the placement. My instructor did not ask any questions; instead, he gave me a new address to visit the next day for an alternative placement.

It was dull work, driving as a team to a residential district and giving out soap samples to ninety different people each day. I worked hard and liked the fact that as soon as we hit the magic number of ninety, we could return to the van and wait out whatever was left of the day.

At first I struggled to make it back on time, but by the end of the first week, after praying hard and refining my sales pitch, I managed to finish two hours ahead of schedule. I made myself comfortable in the back of the van, confirmed that the driver was still dozing in the front, and started to read.

"What's that?" a girl asked when she arrived a half hour after I did.

"The Holy Bible."

"What's it about?"

I looked at her carefully. I didn't recognize her from college, but I chose to take a risk anyway.

"It's about Jesus—how he gave his life and how all of us are sinners because Adam was disobedient. If your sins are heavy and cause you pain, he can forgive you. Jesus came to save."

"Oh!" she said.

"Hey!" The driver sat up, bleary eyed, and turned to the back of the van. "What do you think you're doing? I don't want people talking about things like that in this van."

"But I finished my work!" I protested. "I was just reading and talking."

†

The next week, before the driver parked and let us out, he announced that instead of waiting for us to finish, he would leave right away. "As soon as you're finished, you can all go home."

When the others had stepped out of the van, I spoke with the driver. "Is this because of what happened last week? I was only answering that girl's questions."

"No, you were preaching in the van!" he said. "I heard you. Why would you do that?"

"It's my duty."

"Your duty? With whose permission?"

"With God's permission."

"God gave you permission?"

"Yes, and he gave that permission to all Christians. We're told to go and tell the whole world about him."

"Shut up!"

"What? You asked me a question, and I'm just answering it."

I was not surprised when the boss asked to see me a couple of days later. "You're good at the work," he said, "but if you want to continue, you can't say a single word about your faith. Even if someone asks you about it, you can't say anything."

"I'm sorry, sir. I can't promise that. I will tell the truth if anyone asks me."

"Then go. We're not going to pay you for the first two weeks. But we will forgive you, for Allah's sake."

"I will happily go. And I would gladly offer thousands of dollars at the feet of my Lord. These wages you're withholding from me are a small offering compared to the offering I want to make to my Lord. But thank you for the chance to give to him anyway."

✝

If my first experience of publicly declaring my faith taught me that God would protect me and my second reminded me that I should never compromise my beliefs, my third and final placement made it clear just how right John was when he talked about the passage in Matthew. I was about to discover what it felt like to be truly hated.

For the final week of our placement, I was sent to a business on the edge of the city. The office was run by two men, and one of them, who wore the traditional green turban and long beard of an extremist, took an instant dislike to me.

I walked into the ramshackle office on my first morning and stood in front of a tiny desk while Muhammad Hamza looked me up and down.

"Muslim?" he said.

"No, I'm a Christian."

He flinched a little at this, as if the revelation made him physically sick.

"Why do you have a Muslim name?"

I went into the same explanation I had used before, about my parents liking it, but he cut me off. "You should become a Muslim," he said, a false smile spreading across his face. "It would be better for you."

Caught in his stare, I could not think of what to say.

He put me to work soon after, but at the end of the next day, he called me into his office. His smile was a little less broad this time.

"Jesus is not the Son of God," Hamza said as soon as he shut the door behind me. "You Christians are all following the wrong path. What do you say to that, eh?"

Unlike the previous day, when I had felt tongue-tied, my

voice was full of confidence. "Christians are all children of God because of Jesus Christ."

Hamza's smile vanished instantly. "This is kafir! You Christians are all infidels! Give me a better answer than that."

Help me, Lord, I prayed. *Please guide me.*

I remembered how Daniel responded when he was asked to interpret the king's dream. He asked for time, went home, and prayed with his friends. I did not have friends I could pray with, but I could at least take some time.

"Please, Mr. Hamza," I said. "We are running out of time. The day is almost over, and if I take a long time to reply, I'll be home late. Can we talk about this matter another day?"

At home that night, I joined my family as I did every evening, kneeling on my prayer mat but silently calling out to Jesus Christ. After prayers, I joined my parents and siblings in the TV lounge, where everyone was watching a program about Muslim pilgrims.

"Today," the narrator announced, "millions will perform pilgrimage in Mecca, Saudi Arabia."

That was all I needed to hear. A plan began to form. I closed my eyes and thanked God.

†

I was waiting outside the office the next morning, a newspaper in my hand. "Are you ready to answer my question?" Hamza asked.

"Yes, I am. Why is it wrong for Christians to say they are children of God when Muslims say it themselves?"

"You're wrong." He scowled. "We would never say such a thing. No true Muslim would think it either."

"But Mr. Hamza, when Muslims perform *hajj*, how do people describe it?"

He looked confused, and I handed him the newspaper. It was folded to a piece about pilgrims. "Read that."

Just like the news report the night before, the paper used an Urdu phrase to describe the pilgrims: *Farzandan-e-Toheed.* I knew the phrase well.

"Mr. Hamza, what does *Farzandan* mean?"

"Followers."

"Are you sure? Remember that it is also kafir to change the meaning as it has been written in the Qur'an. Or maybe you were never taught Arabic properly. *Farzandan* comes from a Persian word that means 'son' or 'offspring,' while *Toheed* means 'invisible oneness of God.' That's right, isn't it? I can always bring in my dictionary tomorrow if you think I might be mistaken."

He said nothing.

"Mr. Hamza, many people have invited me to join Islam, just as you did. As a result, I have studied the Qur'an and Islam to know their teachings. After deep research, I know I'm on the right path."

"Who taught you how to read the Qur'an in Arabic so well?"

"If you want to understand physics or mathematics, you hire a tutor. Why can't a Christian hire a teacher to learn the Qur'an?"

He blew out his cheeks and checked his watch. It was time for me to start work, and he indicated I should leave. "Surely you will go to heaven because you know Arabic."

I stopped at the doorway. His nonsense made me even bolder. "Yes, I will go to heaven, but not because I know Arabic. I will go only because I believe in Jesus Christ, who has all authority over heaven and earth. He is my Savior, and he is the Son of Most High God. He gave his life on the cross for my sins and for the sins of all humanity. Because of his sacrifice on the cross, I am free from the bondage of sin. Everyone who believes in his sacrifice is free from their sins."

I took a step toward his desk. "'For God so loved the world that he gave his one and only Son, that whoever believes in him shall not perish but have eternal life.' That is written in the Holy Bible, John 3:16."

He looked at me blankly.

"'He was pierced for our transgressions, he was crushed for our iniquities; the punishment that brought us peace was on him, and by his wounds we are healed.' Isaiah 53:5."

Undeterred, I kept going, my voice growing louder, my heart getting bolder. "'What I received I passed on to you as of first importance: that Christ died for our sins according to the Scriptures.' That's from 1 Corinthians 15:3."

I explained that Jesus Christ is the Son of God and that whoever believes in him will surely have eternal life, but that his patience would only last so long.

"Go," he said. "You're late for work."

†

Hamza never bothered me again after that. In fact, he hardly spoke to me at all. I smiled inside whenever he scuttled away from me in the corridor. I smiled even more when I found out he was a member of a radical Islamic faction. He liked people to think of him as a committed, hard-line believer, but I knew him to be a coward.

The more time I spent debating religion with Muslims, the clearer it became to me that although they wanted to get to heaven, they were blind to the path that would take them there. I'd been no different myself. I had been desperate to get to heaven, not knowing that I was heading straight toward hell. All of that had changed, though. By the grace of my Lord Jesus Christ, I had locked all doors that led to hell and thrown away the keys.

Over the remaining weeks of my placement, I didn't have many opportunities to talk with others about Christianity, although I did manage to study my Bible on the street whenever I was on a break. The only person who disturbed me was the janitor, an old man who didn't mind what I did. He just nodded silently whenever he passed me. When I saw him approaching, I'd hide my book behind an academic textbook, relishing the extra minutes to study and pray.

Two days before my placement was due to end, the old man spoke to me. "You need to be careful of Mr. Hamza," he said. "He's talking about a plan that he and two others have hatched. They're going to rape you tomorrow evening before you leave."

I thanked him and left for home that instant, knowing I would never return. I wasn't panicking or gripped by fear. The whole journey home, I reflected on two of my favorite Scriptures: "If God is for us, who can be against us?"[8] and "Who is going to harm you if you are eager to do good?"[9]

The irony of my placement adventures was not lost on me. I was supposed to return to college having experienced a range of different work environments, acquired new skills, and become better equipped to work as an engineer. I had learned little that could help me in those regards, but as a Christian, I'd acquired some of the most valuable lessons of my life.

I learned that when someone is committed to praying, reading the Holy Bible daily, and spending time in God's presence, then Satan is weak and fearful. He cannot harm us, because God Almighty will protect us. I learned that although Satan seems strong at times, he is no match for Jesus Christ. When we take refuge in him, we must remember that he has defeated Satan and trampled his head with his foot. Jesus Christ is the victor; he is our King. And we are his responsibility.

Most important, I learned that God is an ever-present help for those who call on him. Thanks to Mr. Hamza and the others, I had been presented with vital opportunities to do just that. As a result, the words of Jeremiah 33:3 had soaked deep into my soul: "Call to me and I will answer you and tell you great and unsearchable things you do not know."

I had come through the season of testing with my faith strengthened and my courage increased. Even so, as one set of trials ended, I sensed that another was beginning. But there was no way for me to know that what was coming next would be more challenging than anything I'd experienced yet.

16

My mother brought up the subject of my marriage as casually as if she were asking me to take a trip to the market.

"Your father and I want to go for pilgrimage this year, and you know we're not allowed to make hajj when we have an unmarried, grown daughter at home," she said as I helped her water her vegetables in the garden. "So we want you to get married as soon as possible. We have a good proposal for you already—a very religious man who is as devoted to Allah as you are. I know he will make you happy."

I tried to cover up the terror that was stabbing at my heart. "But I'm twenty-one," was all I could think to say.

She smiled, nodding in agreement. "And I was sixteen when I married. So were both your sisters. Twenty-one is perfect for marriage."

"Please," I said meekly, "let me finish my studies first."

"That isn't my decision to make—it's your father's. Perhaps he'll say yes. I'll discuss it with him."

I had known that something like this was coming. For years I'd been aware of the comments relatives and neighbors made about me, the same way they talked about every unmarried girl my age. In Pakistan, as soon as a girl is old enough to bear a child, she is considered old enough to marry—or at least to have her potential suitability as a bride be discussed loudly in public.

While both my older sisters had married and had children before they were nineteen, I had held fast. My parents had not brought up the subject since I had volunteered for jihad. That suited me well, since even before I became a Christian, I knew that getting married would most likely mean an end to my education. Now that I was living as a secret believer, the stakes were even higher. I did not want to be married to a Muslim, especially not one who was as religious as my parents thought I was. Being a secret believer would be a lot harder with an attentive husband than with an absent father.

This was bigger than I could handle on my own. I needed God to intervene.

†

A few days passed before my mother brought up the subject again.

"Your father said he will discuss arrangements with the man's family."

"No," I said. This time I wasn't terrified; I was enraged. Having spent too many hours imagining the horrors of being forced to marry a fanatical Muslim, I was ready to fight against my parents' plan. "I don't want to get married. I want to continue my studies."

My mother started to speak but stopped herself. Her eyes shot past my shoulder. I turned and saw my father standing in the kitchen doorway.

Even though we lived in the same house, he and I had become strangers. We hardly ever spoke, and I couldn't remember the last time we'd been alone in the same room together. Whenever he was home, he stayed in the drawing room or the meeting room downstairs. He never came into the kitchen, and he never called me by name.

"Zakhira." At the sound of his voice, my anger diffused, only to be replaced by fear. "It's not your choice. If your husband allows, you can continue your studies. But if he says no, then you won't. He'll be the one to decide. You're a woman. What else do you need to be able to do besides the cooking and cleaning?"

I could not say anything in reply. His presence left me mute.

I did not bring up the matter again. One time my mother explained why I should be happy, reminding me that when both my sisters had married, my father had given them some of the biggest dowries people had ever heard of. They had enough money to buy everything they wanted for their homes, plus there was lots of gold for my sisters, jewelry for their husbands, and expensive gifts for the grooms' mothers. "With an offer like that, we can choose from the very best families. Isn't that good?"

I continued my silent protest, even after my mother told me they had heard from the man's family on the subject of my continued education.

"You have nothing to worry about," my mother said. "After getting married, you can continue your studies. Isn't that good news?"

It was the very worst news. My attempts at stalling the

process had failed. It would be impossible for me to practice my Christian faith while married to a militant Muslim man. And if he found out the truth, he would surely divorce me—or kill me.

When I realized just how powerless and weak I was, I did what I should have done all along. I bowed down in prayer, my heart contrite. I begged God for a solution.

He gave it to me right away.

It was time to tell my mother the truth.

†

I told her in the prayer room. We were alone in the house after finishing our second prayers for the day. As we rolled up our mats, I took a deep breath and told her I was no longer a Muslim. "I'm a faithful Christian now. If you really want me to get married, I will only marry a Christian man."

I harbored a tiny hope that she might understand. Perhaps she would say that we could talk to my father together, that she would help me try to explain it all.

Instead she looked at me in horror. "This means the letter you wrote asking for the Bible was true?"

"Yes. I didn't want a Holy Bible so I could become a better Muslim. I wanted one because I'm a follower of Jesus now."

She froze. Her eyes were so fierce that I had to look away. When she spoke, her voice trembled with anger. "I knew something was wrong when that business with the letter happened. Who made you a Christian? Who taught you all these things? Was it those women who visited?"

"It started when Anwar told me that the stories of the prophets can be found in the Holy Bible. From that time on, I've been searching on my own. No one else has been involved."

"Why are you doing this?" Her eyes searched me, pleading. "I'm your mother. Why are you trying to make a fool of me?"

"I'm not. I just can't turn my back on the truth."

"The truth? You mean Islam is not a true religion?"

"No, it's not. Only Christianity is the true path that leads to God, heaven, and everlasting life."

Her hand shot out and slapped my cheek. Another blow landed on the other side of my head. I tried to block her, but one of her hands clenched around my wrist while the other clamped onto my jaw. She was squeezing so tight I could feel pain in every cell.

She pulled me close, spitting out the words. "Your father won't spare you at all. He will surely kill you."

When she slacked her grip on my jaw, I looked directly at her. "I know. I'm ready."

In my room alone, after the adrenaline had faded a little from my body, I opened my Holy Bible. I knew what passage I wanted to read, and my fingers found their way to the right page almost automatically. "Blessed are those who are persecuted because of righteousness, for theirs is the kingdom of heaven. Blessed are you when people insult you, persecute you and falsely say all kinds of evil against you because of me. Rejoice and be glad, because great is your reward in heaven, for in the same way they persecuted the prophets who were before you."[10]

Those words had drawn me like a magnet ever since I read them in John's lab, long before I became a Christian. John had been careful to point out the verses to me, making sure I understood them. He told me that Christians are often persecuted, just as Jesus said they would be. He told me that people would hate me, despise me, possibly even try to kill me.

I looked at the bruise that was beginning to form on my

right wrist. I felt the swelling in my mouth from where I had been hit. The physical marks were painful, but the pain only went so deep. Beneath the pain was something far stronger: peace. My mother's reaction reminded me that the Holy Bible really is true. Yes, I was bruised, and there was good reason to fear what might happen tomorrow. But this was not the end of the story. I had been beaten for my faith in Jesus. That meant I was blessed.

†

My mother woke me the next morning to pray with her and my sister. I did as she told me, offering my silent *Hallelujah!* while she and my sister filled the room with "Allahu Akbar." After we finished, she sent my sister out to begin her chores. She watched me as I rolled up my mat.

"If you're a Christian, why are you even offering prayers like this?"

"The Holy Bible says, 'Honor your father and your mother, so that you may live long'[11] and 'Children, obey your parents in the Lord, for this is right.'[12] So that's what I'm doing."

She threw up her hands. "Don't touch this prayer mat! You're making things unclean."

"My heart is with the Lord. You can't take the name of Jesus Christ out of my heart and mind."

She pulled out her prayer beads, knelt down on her mat again, and started to chant quietly. She was quoting verses from the Qur'an, but I chose not to listen.

I prayed instead. *Lord Jesus Christ, whatever my mother is reciting for me, I ask you to remove and destroy the effects in your holy name. You have purchased me with your holy blood, and now I am yours. I take refuge in you. In Jesus Christ's most powerful name I say this. Amen.*

The beatings continued after that day, growing steadily worse. My mother would wait until we were alone in a room, and then she'd grab me by the throat and squeeze so tightly I could not breathe.

"I'm going to kill you," she would say, her eyes spiked with hate. "I'll kill you in the name of Allah, and that will put things right again."

I could not make a sound, but I prayed inside, committing everything to God. *I'm ready to pay the price. You paid it for me already, and I am yours. You can do with me whatever you want.*

It was hard to see my mother's feelings toward me change so quickly from love to hatred, and it left me with immense sorrow. I felt no animosity toward her, only pity, knowing that Satan had covered her eyes.

Besides, I was fully aware of my own sin. I had been willing to kill God's people, and yet he'd chosen to welcome me into his family. He had rescued me—a sinner. He picked me from the trash, washed me with his blood, and made me a new person. What right did I have to stand upright before God? He was so pure and so clean and so innocent. My body and my life were nothing. Even if every last drop of my blood got poured onto the ground, it would not come close to atoning for all I had done wrong. I owed God everything.

"Ami," I said as the air returned to my body, "I'm telling you the truth. If you cut me into pieces, each piece of my body will say, 'Jesus Christ is my Lord and Savior.'"

†

As the days passed, my mother turned into even more of a monster. Her face would twist in rage as she shouted at me. Her grip on my throat grew tighter and lasted longer each time, and her blows to my forearm came down heavier and more frequently. After a few days, she started using other weapons, first hitting me with shoes, then with a cane.

She always attacked me in places that were covered by my clothes and dupatta—mainly my arm and my throat. Within a week, I could not use my right hand or swallow without shooting pains. At night I dreamed that my hand was on fire. Yet I told myself that this was nothing compared to what Jesus experienced. I cried whenever I read about the crucifixion of Jesus. Knowing that he was innocent, that he came from a higher place to save our lives, that he took the lashes he did not deserve—this perspective changed how I felt about my own trials. What I faced wasn't so bad. Compared to the thorns, the nails, the whippings, the spitting, and the taunts Jesus endured, this was nothing.

The more I thought about what Jesus went through on my behalf, the more determined I became to suffer well for my Lord.

†

Ever since John gave me the Holy Bible, I had been careful to move its hiding place regularly. I had more than a dozen spots where I was confident it would remain undetected—among my clothes, in the darkest corners of the kitchen, behind heavy furniture that was never moved.

I would get it out at night and read it alone in my bedroom. Almost every night I turned to these words Paul wrote: "I consider that our present sufferings are not worth comparing with the glory that will be revealed in us."[13]

One day I opened the book of Esther and read about her decision to offer a three-day fast. I was struck by how God radically changed the situation after that. I wanted the same outcome as my namesake—for God to turn someone's murderous intent into a glorious example of his love and power. I was desperate for him to act.

Lord, I prayed, *I learned how to love from you. Despite who I was—someone who was ready to kill your people—you looked at me in love and gave me joy and life. I learned love from you even though I was a sinful girl. You saved me. I didn't deserve any of this goodness. Even though Mom is hurting me, I still love her with the love you gave me.*

I decided to fast for three days. My mother grew worried when I refused all food and water, asking me if I was on a hunger strike in an attempt to punish her. I stayed firm, telling her I did not want anything at all from her.

On the morning of the third day, I was praying in the darkness of my room when I heard the Lord's gentle whisper: *When you're talking with your mother, I am with you. My Spirit is speaking through you.*

I started to cry. *Lord, thank you,* I prayed. *When you appeared to Saul, you changed him radically. I believe my mother will also change. And God, please heal her from the physical pain she is in.*

I heard the Lord's voice again: *I will increase her pain, and she will call on me herself. Then she will be healed. This disease is to glorify my name.*

✝

It was easy to change the way I spoke to my mother. I no longer felt the need to defend myself against her or to avoid all but essential contact with her. I saw her not as someone who was persecuting me but as a fellow traveler soon to be invited onto the path of God's great adventure.

I asked her again and again if I could pray for her. I didn't mind when she shouted at me to leave or pushed me away. I just wanted her to know I was ready to pray for her, ready to believe that God would heal her and that his name would be glorified as a result.

She showed no sign of backing down, but her beatings slowed a little in both their frequency and their force. I wondered whether this was a sign that God was at work within her, but I knew there was another explanation to consider as well. She had been told by the doctor that the problem with her heart was rapidly getting worse and that her health would continue to deteriorate. Without any female surgeons in the city, both she and my father continued to refuse an operation. The longer she lived with her condition, the worse she became.

We were out shopping one day when my mother collapsed on the sidewalk beside me. One moment she was looking at fruit, and the next she lay twisted on the ground, surrounded by fallen mangoes.

I forgot all about the miracle I had been praying for and knelt beside her, desperate to do what I could to help. Her hands grabbed at my dupatta, and when she'd pulled me close enough to her face for me to hear her faint, rasping voice, she spoke. "You pray."

A bunch of people gathered around and helped me move her off to the side. I sat there as her head rested limply in my lap, her eyes wide. I'd never seen her so scared.

"Lord, you said that she would ask for healing herself, and she has done just that. So please heal my mother." She shut her eyes as I continued to pray. "Jesus, I bring her under your cross. I cover her with your holy blood. Whatever sickness is inside her body, remove it in your mighty name, Jesus."

For a while we sat there like that, my mother lying in the dirt and the name of Jesus fresh on my lips while the rest of Pakistan went about its business around us. It seemed like the most normal thing in the world.

When I noticed that her face had relaxed and her breathing had calmed, I told her I wanted to call home and get my father to pick her up.

She opened her eyes and stared straight at me. "I have no pain," she said. "I'm ready to go straight to the hospital."

My father and brother came and drove us to the same building where I'd visited John so many times before. As I waited in the corridor while the doctor and nurses examined her, I felt an odd mixture of emotions. I wasn't sure what was happening with my mother's health, and I wondered how God would answer my prayer. At the same time, I was nervous that I might see John again, afraid that in the midst of all the chaos, he might somehow get found out and end up in trouble. Even so, part of me was desperate to walk up to the second floor and see him again. Months had passed since we last saw each other, and I had so much to tell him.

"It's a miracle," the doctor said as he stood beside my mother in the open doorway. "There's nothing wrong with her heart at all!"

My father rejoiced and my brother hugged my mother while silent prayers of joy exploded within me. The only person who was not smiling or cheering was my mother. She stood still, her eyes fixed on the floor.

Later that night, when the house had cleared of guests and noise, I heard a soft knock on my door. My mother came in and sat on my bed, looking at her hands. She said nothing for a long time.

"I had such a strange experience when you started praying," she said. "I saw fire."

I desperately wanted to tell her that fire was a Christian concept—to share about Moses and the burning bush and the disciples on the day of Pentecost. I wanted to tell her that there could be only one possible explanation for her dramatic healing. I wanted to tell her everything about Jesus and the time I'd fasted and prayed and how he had promised to heal her. But I knew I couldn't. Not yet, anyway. So I just stared at her hands too and waited for the moment to pass.

Finally she found the words she wanted to speak. "I heard the sound of a stone falling down. Then the pain vanished. That's why I wanted to go straight to the hospital. I knew that my problem was gone. I just wanted proof."

"You know who healed you, don't you?"

She said nothing, just stared at her hands.

Before I could ask the question a second time, she stood up and left.

17

That day in the market was not the first time I'd seen Jesus heal someone. It wasn't even the first time I had seen him heal my mother.

It happened over a decade earlier, before I started at the madrassa. I walked in after school one day and noticed that something was out of place. On the shelf in the hall that held my trophies, certificates, and A-grade tests was an additional item that had not been there when I left in the morning. There on the shelf, between my first debate trophy and a report card on which my teacher praised me for being the most diligent pupil in the school, was a single piece of paper, carefully folded.

I was on the verge of asking my mother about it when curiosity took over. I opened the paper, fold by fold, until it was bigger than my hand. Just two words were written on it in Arabic script: *Jesu Shafi*.

The names were vaguely familiar, but the pairing struck me as odd. I knew that *Shafi* was an Arabic name that could mean a number of things. Mediator. Truthful. Healer. *Jesu* I was less familiar with. Wasn't that the name some people called Isa, one of the prophets? But why put them together? And why was it on my trophy shelf?

I went in search of my mother, waving the paper above my head. Before I could say anything, she gasped and closed her eyes.

"Zakhira! Why did you open it?"

"It was on my shelf."

"Did you read it?"

"Yes. It says—"

"Don't!" she shouted. "The mullah said we must not read it if we want it to work. Fold it up and put it back."

She sat down, clutching her jaw. It struck me that she looked old and tired.

I sat beside her, leaning my head on her shoulder. "I'm really sorry, Ami."

"It's not your fault, Zakhira. I have a toothache and I couldn't sleep last night, so I went to the mosque and asked one of the mullahs for help. He gave me the paper and told me not to open it but to wear it around my neck. I was waiting to go to the market to ask the cobbler to sew it into a leather pouch for me."

"Oh," I said. "Will it not work now?"

"I don't know."

When my father came home and heard what had happened, he took us all to the mosque right away. It was the first time I could remember going to the mosque with my father, and as we waited in a corridor, I sat silent and still, happy for the covering my veil provided.

The mullah listened carefully as my father explained what had happened. Then he asked my mother if she had read the paper.

"No," she said.

"And did you read it?" he asked me.

"Yes," I said, too quietly at first. At my father's prodding, I spoke a little louder. "Yes! I read it."

To my surprise, the mullah was not angry. He simply looked at me, waved his hand, and told my father that I was still young and not yet mature, so there was no problem. "You can still use it," he said to my mother. "But keep it close to you."

†

I had not thought about the incident for years—not until I became a Christian and was able to look at the Qur'an through new eyes. The more of this book I read, the more I understood that the prophet written about as Isa and known the world over as Jesus was a healer. It was to Jesus, the Son of God, that the mullah had turned for help. And it was Jesus who had delivered rapid and complete healing of my mother's toothache soon after I read the note.

Ever since my mother had started beating me, I'd been desperate to remind her of the episode. When my mother was healed of her heart condition, I was confident the opportunity would soon arise.

The trouble was, once she was healed, she went quiet on me. For days she avoided all but the most basic of conversations with me. When I went to sit beside her, she would get up and move away. I was glad that the violence had stopped, but I longed to talk with her. I wanted to hear all about what had happened when I prayed, to know what kinds of questions she was asking. I wanted to talk to her about Jesus and share some of my journey with her.

Instead, she locked me out. Whatever was going on inside her, she did not want to share it with me.

It took three weeks for my mother to break the silence. I was alone in my room one evening, praying on the floor. She came in without knocking, quietly closed the door behind her, and sat on my bed. After wanting to talk for so long, I found myself struggling to find the words to start.

She spoke first. "Your brother is sick," she said. "His leg is infected, and the doctor says that if the infection reaches the bone, they will have to amputate."

The news came as a shock. I knew he'd been laid up in bed for a while, but I had no idea what the problem was or that the outlook was so serious. I felt bad for having been so caught up in my own thoughts that I hadn't wondered what was going on with everyone else in the house.

All at once a thought cast a shadow across my mind. Maybe the reason for my mother's silence was not that she was in the middle of a crisis of faith or that she was thinking about Jesus. Maybe she was in denial about the miraculous healing and would never talk about what had happened.

"I want you to pray for your brother," she said.

I wanted to shout, "Yes!" and run into his room at that very moment. But different words came out of my mouth—ones I hadn't planned on saying. "Do you really believe that Jesus can hear my prayers?"

"Yes."

"And do you believe that Jesus can heal?"

"Yes," she said, tears filling her eyes. "The last time you prayed, my problem went away. If you pray now, I believe Jesus will heal him."

"Ami, if we both believe that Jesus can heal, why don't we both pray?"

The tears flowed fast. Between sobs, she gulped great lung-fuls of air. It took several minutes before she was able to speak again.

"Will Jesus hear me? Even though I beat you? Won't he be angry?"

"No," I said. "Every day he's waiting for you. His arms are always open."

She wiped her face and looked up. "I will pray with you."

I took my Holy Bible from its hiding place and opened it to Matthew 18, where Jesus promises that if two of his follow-ers agree about anything and ask for it, our Father in heaven will answer that prayer.

I went to the kitchen for some mustard oil. My mother looked confused when I showed it to her, but she followed me to my brother's room and listened as I prayed.

"Lord Jesus, this is no longer oil but your blood that was shed to heal our pain and our diseases and to remove our sins. It is sufficient for this wound, and it is better than any medi-cine or ointment in this world."

I handed the bottle over to her and told her to apply it to the wound while my brother slept, saying the same prayer I had said.

By the next morning, my brother's wound had started to shrink. She continued praying and rubbing. Within a week, the wound had healed completely and my brother was well.

†

"I have seen two miracles happen before my own eyes," my mother said when we were working in the garden one morn-ing. "But I'm confused. If Jesus Christ is true and there really is healing power in his name, why did Allah send Hazrat Muhammad as the greatest prophet among all prophets? Why should the Bible, which tells about the lives of the prophets like Moses and Jesus, be abolished? And why did Allah send Hazrat Muhammad with the Qur'an to show us the right way?"

I stopped digging. "The books in the Bible are not abolished. The Qur'an confirms that those books are true."

"That's not what the clerics teach. They say that the books in the Bible aren't permitted."

"What should you trust more: the words of the Qur'an or the words of a cleric? According to your faith, the Qur'an is from Allah. Any cleric is human, just like you or me. And we all make mistakes, don't we?"

She nodded.

"If you really believe in the Qur'an, I will show you what's written in it. Wait here." I ran inside to find my Qur'an, its pages covered with highlighter marks, its spine cracked from study. I told her which passages to look up to find out how the Qur'an describes Jesus—as the son of the virgin Mary, as one who performed miracles nobody else could perform, as the man who could raise the dead—and as she read each one, I asked her to read not just the original Arabic but also the Urdu translations printed on the side.

I dug my fingers into the soil as she read, thinking about the ways the clerics had blinded my mother, just as they'd done to almost every other Muslim I knew. They discouraged people from reading in anything other than Arabic, and they so often appealed to the emotions of hatred and fear. Too few Muslims knew that the Qur'an has plenty to say about Jesus. If they would just read with their own eyes, they would see that Islam offers no guarantees about life after death.

My mother was quiet when she finished reading. Just then my brother called from the house, putting an end to our discussion. I desperately needed wisdom and knowledge in order to answer her questions, and for the rest of the day this Scripture repeated in my head: "If any of you lacks wisdom, you should ask God, who gives generously to all without finding fault, and it will be given to you."[14]

Two days later, I had my answer. As I was looking through a collection of Islamic books my father owned, I found one I knew would help. I invited my mother to sit with me in my room and reminded her of her question about why Muhammad is above all prophets.

"Listen to this," I said, opening up the book *Dua Ganjul Arsh*.

There is no creature or entity worthy of worship except
    for Allah,
  Adam, who was the chosen of Allah,
There is no creature or entity worthy of worship except
    for Allah,
  Nuh [Noah], the saved of Allah,
There is no creature or entity worthy of worship except
    for Allah,
  Ibrahim [Abraham], the friend of Allah,
There is no creature or entity worthy of worship except
    for Allah,
  Ismail [Ishmael], the sacrificed of Allah,
There is no creature or entity worthy of worship except
    for Allah,
  Musa [Moses], the one who spoke to Allah,
There is no creature or entity worthy of worship except
    for Allah,

Dawud [David], the successor of Allah (on his earth),
There is no creature or entity worthy of worship except
    for Allah,
Isa (Jesus), the Spirit of Allah,
There is no creature or entity worthy of worship except
    for Allah,
Muhammad is the messenger of Allah.

"Tell me honestly—did you hear anything that says Muhammad is chief?"

"No."

I opened my Qur'an, turning to the verse John had shown me the day I first met him in the lab: "I'm no new thing among the messengers [of Allah], nor know I what will be done with me or with you. I do but follow that which is inspired in me, and I am but a plain Warner."

I let the words rest in the air awhile, remembering the impact they'd had on me when I first read them. "Muhammad is just a simple messenger—nothing more than that. He doesn't even know what will happen on the day of judgment. But look at the Holy Bible, and you'll see that Jesus is confident when he promises eternal life even after death."

I showed her John 11:25 and read the words of Jesus: "I am the resurrection and the life. The one who believes in me will live, even though they die."

"Do you see what all this means? God was fully in Isa—in Jesus. That's the reason Jesus can talk about the future with confidence—because he is fully God. He is God in human flesh, and he is still at work today."

"Yes," she said, staring at nothing in particular. I was desperate to say more, just like I was desperate for her to have the same revelation about Jesus that I'd had. But whatever was going on within my mother, it was not up to me to control. I watched her eyebrows furrow before she abruptly stood up and left.

†

Our conversation about Jesus spread out over many weeks. It was like a game of chess, where the players consider each move carefully before laying a finger on their pieces. Though I was desperate to have my mother give her life over to Jesus as I had done, I knew I could not rush her. I vowed to be as patient with her as John had been with me. In the days between our discussions, I did what I was sure John had done: I prayed.

When she finally came to my room one night, I'd been asleep for hours. The air was a little cold, and I listened as she whispered her thoughts about Jesus.

"I know there is power in the name of Jesus," she said. "Even his name written on a scrap of paper was enough to heal me of my toothache."

I reached out and touched her arm. "I remember that too," I said. "I didn't know whether you remembered it."

She smiled. "I've hardly thought about anything else for the last few weeks." She shivered a little in the cold, and I offered her a blanket. She waved it away. Silence returned to the room.

"Zakhira-jan, how can I become a Christian?"

A thousand candles ignited within me. I could feel both of our tears on our cheeks as I hugged her.

"You start by saying that you're sorry. Repeat after me: 'I know that I have done wrong. Please forgive me, and forgive my sins.'"

She stiffened beside me. Fear twitched across her face. "Oh, no. I'm not a sinner. I've never done any sins."

"We're all born sinners."

"What do you mean? That I sinned and then you were born?"

"No, but Adam committed sin. Even the Qur'an tells us that. We are all born with sin, and that's why Jesus came to save us."

I told her about the woman whose bleeding made her unclean and how Jesus hadn't turned her away. I talked about Peter's denials and his later restoration, and about David's mistakes and repentance in Psalm 51. "You tried everything, didn't you? All the shrines, all the prayer beads. But only the name of Jesus brought you close to the healing power of God. Even when you were years away from believing in him, when you didn't know you were wearing his Son's name around your neck, he was ready to show you how much he loves you. So yes, we're all sinners and we all need saving, but the love of Jesus is big enough to bring us in. We just have to admit what we've done wrong."

She nodded slowly, taking it all in. There was no flicker of doubt in her eyes.

"I know I've done wrong," she said, repeating the words I offered. "Please forgive me, and forgive my sins. I believe that I'm saved now. You have purchased me by your holy sacrifice. You have given your holy and sinless body and blood as a precious sacrifice for me. You died on the cross, you were buried, and on the third day you were resurrected from the grave. And now you are alive and always with us. I surrender my life to you. Amen."

Part 3

DO NOT WORRY ABOUT WHAT YOU WILL SAY

18

"Amen," I said, opening my eyes. My mother and I were kneeling in the garden, our backs to the house and our dusty hands resting on our laps.

Two weeks had passed since my mother turned her back on Islam and embraced Christianity, and every morning since, we'd met to pray before I went to my college classes. As I knelt in the dirt, I noticed the signs of growth among the chilies and tomatoes, the mint and the coriander. I could not image a more perfect place to meet with God each day to ask forgiveness and plead with him for strength and hope.

My mother's eyes remained shut. "Amen," I said again, a little louder this time. Her shoulders slumped when I reached out to touch her. "Ami, are you okay?"

"Last night your father said that you have to get married this summer. He said he won't wait any longer. I didn't know what to say to him."

I was not surprised. It was inevitable that he would want me to marry, and my mother was just as powerless as I was to stop him. But I wasn't gripped by despair. After all, when I explained to my mother why I could not marry, it had eventually led to her becoming a Christian. Could the same thing happen with my father?

"It's okay," I said. "It's better that we tell him the truth about me."

A look of terror crossed her face.

"Don't worry, Ami. God's mighty power is more than enough for both of us."

†

The next morning, there was no time to pray in the garden. Even before I got out of bed, the house was filled with my father's rage. "Why does she want to marry a Christian?" he shouted.

My mother's voice was too soft for me to hear, but my father's reply left no doubt that she had told him about my conversion.

"I'll kill her!"

"No!" My mother's voice rose. "She's done nothing wrong."

"Nothing wrong? She's an infidel! A few months ago, she brought all that embarrassment on me by asking for a Bible. How will I face people when they find out about this? How will I answer their questions?"

"Let them ask their questions of her, and let her give her own replies."

He said nothing, but I heard his feet pound up the stairs. Before I knew it, he'd flung open my door. He paused for a moment, staring at me as I sat on my bed. When I registered the hatred in his eyes, I felt sick inside.

"Come back to Islam. Otherwise I'll forget you are my daughter. I'll slaughter you in the name of Allah."

I stood up, and words rose within me like a summer cyclone. They were unexpected and sudden, and there was nothing I could do to stop them. For the first time in my life, I stepped toward my father, looked him in the eye, and told him the truth. "I have burned the boats of Islam. It's impossible for me to choose a way that has no destination and no promise of eternal life. Jesus Christ has opened a door of eternal life for me. I'm looking forward, not back. I love Jesus Christ. He is my first love."

My father's beard twitched. I'd seen that happen before. Everyone in the house knew this was a sign to take cover, but I stood my ground.

When the slap came moments later, it was harder and more painful than I thought possible. My cheek burned, my jaw pulsed in agony, and it took all my strength to stand upright.

He hit me again—even harder this time. I staggered under the force of the blow, tripping back onto the bed. "You got crazy," he spat. "I know how to handle crazy people."

Then he left my room, pushing past my mother in the doorway. "From now on, she is forbidden from going to college!" he shouted. "She stays at home until she gets married." I heard him slam the front door and walk outside.

I sat and listened to my father's car speed down the street. When I finally lost all trace of its sound, I fell into my mother's arms and wept.

†

I could not have gone to college that day even if I had been allowed to. It was almost impossible to concentrate on anything other than what my father planned to do to me. I found it hard to imagine him keeping me home and forcing me to get married. His threats of killing me seemed far more likely.

He wouldn't have been the first father in the neighborhood to kill his daughter. When I was about twelve, there was a girl on our street named Tamira. She was just four years older than I was, and though we never went to the same school and her family never attended the daras at our home, I knew her a little and liked her. She would always stop, smile, and talk with me when I saw her in the street.

Tamira was sixteen when her father murdered her.

He told the police that it was suicide. They accepted his explanation, even though everyone knew he was lying. A few weeks earlier, Tamira had fallen in love with a boy. When Tamira's father caught her talking to the boy from her bedroom window one night, he decided to act. For a girl to be seen behaving in such a lewd way in public was a major dishonor. So he tied one end of a rope to her neck and the other to a ceiling fan.

When news broke of the boy's death soon after, my mother told me that unlike Tamira's, his death really was a suicide. I did not understand at first. Why would Tamira's father want to murder her but the boy's father didn't need to kill his son?

"Because the girl's sin was greater," my mother said.

†

I thought about Tamira a lot that day. I wondered whether my father would hang me, too. Perhaps he was out buying rope that very afternoon. Would he try to cover up my death, or would he want to make a public example of me, proving to all his friends what a good Muslim he was? Would he believe that he would be rewarded by Allah if he killed me?

I tried helping my mother with her chores. Both of us

prepared food in silence, but I quickly gave up. My hands just would not work the way they were supposed to. As I headed upstairs to pray, a great ache grew within me.

I sat on my bed and cried out to God, the tears flowing freely. A while later, my mother joined me, and we both cried for a long time.

"I don't know what he'll do," she said. "We have to be ready for him to do anything."

"It's okay, Ami. I'm ready."

"No. I gave birth to you. How could I stand by and watch him cut you into pieces as if he were a butcher? How can I pray when this terrible pain is growing inside me?"

She was right. It would be worse for her to watch my torture than it would be for me to endure it. I would soon be with God—maybe even before the sun set that night. The only thing that stood between me and being in the presence of my Savior was pain. And my Savior knew all about pain.

"Whatever I suffer, I want you to remember this one thing: Jesus has suffered more than I ever will," I said. "I can't imagine how painful it must have been for him to hang from nails on a cross. Think about how he endured all those insults and whippings, even though he had the authority to stop them. Remember that it's an honor to suffer because of him. It means he considers me ready to go through this."

We sat in silence for a long time. Finally, when the sun started to fade in the window, my mother stood up to leave. "Your father will be home soon," she said. "I need to be downstairs when he arrives."

†

It had been dark for a long time when the crowd gathered in the street. Judging by her eyes, my mother had been crying for hours as well. But the moment we embraced in the doorway, with the orange streetlight and the restless crowd just beyond us, everything stopped.

There, in the smell of her hair—a mixture of jasmine and almonds—and the soft, familiar feel of her cheek pressed against mine, I was at peace. I needed nothing else in life. To hug Ami was enough.

But I also knew that God had already done so much in our lives. He had rescued both of us. And now I was ready to die.

"Send her out!" My father's voice was insistent. My arms obeyed as I slowly let go of my mother and followed my father onto the street.

I stared at my father as the mob pressed in on all sides. Every time they called for my blood, I watched for his reaction. Nothing would happen unless he said so.

What would he say? It was impossible to tell. As far as he was concerned, I was as good as gone already.

"I have a better idea," he said after the crowd had run out of ideas for how to kill me. The voices fell silent, and I watched as people parted for my father to walk through. Then I saw him pause to talk to a mullah. I recognized him instantly. It was Anwar.

My father returned to the center of the crowd, Anwar at his side. Neither of them looked at me as they spoke.

"Someone has brainwashed this girl," Anwar said. "We'll give her time. One month should be enough for the scholars to see who has been talking to her. If she doesn't come back to Islam then—"

"I will kill her myself," my father said. "I will call all of you standing here tonight, and you will see me do it."

The crowd cheered and shouted their agreement as I was bundled back inside my house.

By the time I was in my bed, the street was nearly empty again, and the noise had dropped to a low hum. I thought about my father's words—how the scholars would come and ask me to explain myself. At some point they'd decide there was no chance of winning me back to Islam. Then I would be taken back to the street to die.

The thought of facing the scholars was even more daunting than the thought of facing my father. What could I possibly say to them that would do justice to my Lord Jesus? How could I, a Christian of less than two years who had never even been inside a church and knew only a few other Christians on this planet, hope to give an account of what it means to be a Christian? I had met Jesus in a dream, and I'd been taught to question Islam by a man whose identity I'd vowed to keep secret. Would any of the scholars take me seriously?

I knew they wouldn't. I knew I was powerless.

I spent the next morning in my room, praying and reading the Holy Bible. My mother brought me food, and I left only to visit the bathroom. Part of me felt like a prisoner. Part of me felt like this was the only place I could be safe.

In the afternoon, when my father came into my room to explain what was going to happen to me, he stood in the doorway while my mother sat beside me on the bed. He addressed all his comments to my mother, asking her to pass on the message to me, as if she were the only one who could communicate with me. In a way, he was right. I smiled inside at the secret that my mother and I shared.

I looked up and tried to catch my father's eye, but he would not—could not?—lay eyes on me. I thought about how little had changed in his view of me in the twenty-one years since I'd been born.

The plan was simple. He had arranged for a female scholar

named Fatima to see me the next morning at ten. She would visit with me in the meeting room, answer any questions I had, and ask some questions of her own. And there would be an audience.

I started fasting at that moment. No food or water passed my lips for the rest of the day, and I decided not to eat or drink until I'd stood up in front of the scholar and whoever else would be there. If I wanted to speak boldly about my faith in Jesus Christ, I would need God's strength to do it.

As the hunger and thirst started to build within me, my prayers grew bolder. I thanked God for choosing me, for the dream I'd had, and for the way he'd guided me to him through Azia, John, and the women who knocked on my door to talk about Jesus. I thanked him for healing my mother and my brother, and for welcoming my mother to himself. I thanked him for his grace, for his love, and for the hope of eternal life. I thanked him for his blood that had been shed and for his death on the cross, which had set me free from the bondage of sin. And I thanked him for this situation I now found myself in.

"But, Lord," I prayed, "I don't know what I should say to that woman. She's a scholar, and I don't know anything. I'm just a child. There's nothing I can say that will change her mind. I'm worried I'll let you down. So I place Fatima in your hands. Will you handle her and deal with her?

"If it's your will for her to come tomorrow, then let it be so. Let the people know that you are the Lord God in heaven and on earth. Lord Jesus, if you want me to die, then I am ready. My life is already yours. You have purchased me by paying the heavy price of your own body. You are the owner of my life, not me. Whenever you want to, you can take it back. Lord

Jesus, there's one thing I know: I love you because you first loved me, even though I was a sinner.

"If they kill me tomorrow, I'm going to be so happy to be coming to you. I am yours. I surrender everything before you. In the everlasting name of Jesus Christ, amen."

†

I did not sleep at all that night. There were some moments when I was able to pray, my faith strong within me. But in other moments, the feeling of loneliness was too much to take. The tears came so fast they stung my eyes, and it was all I could do to suck in enough air between sobs.

A little after 3 a.m., I was lying on my bed, trying to ward off another wave of tears, when I heard a gentle whisper from my Lord. *My daughter, do not say, "I'm just a child." You must go to everyone I send you to and say whatever I command you to say. Don't be afraid of them, for I am with you. I will rescue you.*

I felt the energy return to my body immediately. I got up, said amen, and turned on the light. I took out my Holy Bible and opened it to a page with a bookmark I didn't remember placing there. I read from the book of Jeremiah:

The word of the LORD came to me, saying,

"Before I formed you in the womb I knew you,
 before you were born I set you apart;
 I appointed you as a prophet to the nations."

"Alas, Sovereign LORD," I said, "I do not know how to speak; I am too young."

But the LORD said to me, "Do not say, 'I am too young.' You must go to everyone I send you to

and say whatever I command you. Do not be afraid
of them, for I am with you and will rescue you,"
declares the LORD.

JEREMIAH 1:4-8

The tears returned again, but this time they weren't tears
of fear or sorrow. They were tears of joy and thanksgiving.
They pointed to my deep gratitude to God for confirming so
clearly—and so quickly—what he'd whispered to me.

I was at peace.

Whatever was about to happen, I knew I could trust that
God was leading me. Whatever I would say, I could speak with
confidence and courage. And whatever happened after that I
could leave to God.

If the coming sunrise signaled the start of my last day on
earth, then I would spend every breath and every heartbeat of
that day in service to my Lord.

19

My father took me downstairs at ten in the morning, two hours after I heard the first people arrive. By the time I entered the meeting room, there were so many people packed inside that I had to choose each step with care. One hundred sets of eyes watched my every move as I made my way toward the three women who sat near the front, shrouded in black veils.

When you live in Pakistan and—in public, at least—every part of a woman is covered up except her eyes, you learn to recognize someone from the faintest clues, such as the shape of an eye, the tilt of a head, or the way she holds her hands. I greeted my mother and sister as I sat down beside them, and then I turned to the third woman. I was pretty sure I hadn't met Fatima before, but I looked carefully at the slit that revealed her eyes, wondering if I knew her.

In the two years I'd been living as a secret believer, I'd obeyed my father whenever he told me to attend the daras at home. Most of the time I sat and prayed silently to God, allowing the words of the mullah to slide right past me. But other times the daras was a women-only event, and the atmosphere was less like a lecture hall and more like a living room. We were encouraged to ask questions, and on more than one occasion I asked about the Qur'an. I was always careful not to reveal my true feelings about Islam, but I couldn't help feeling that if Fatima and I had met before, she might use what I'd said against me.

"May I get you a glass of water before we begin?" I asked her.

She said yes. Her voice was unfamiliar, and as I picked my way across the floor, I silently praised God. Once I was alone in the kitchen, I got on my knees and told God for the hundredth time how desperate I was not to let him down. "You know that I've never had to defend my Christian faith in front of scholars before. What do I know? I'm a baby Christian. And like any baby, I'm dependent on the one who gave me life. I'm relying on you to bind Fatima's brain, in your Son's name. Be glorified here today, so that my death will not be for nothing."

†

By the time Fatima stood up to speak, not only was the entire room packed but the courtyard was also filled with people. They crowded around the windows, straining to hear the proceedings.

"Zakhira." Fatima's voice was warm and gentle, full of kindness. It was as if she were admonishing me for missing a couple of questions on a test or failing to attend a daras. "What happened to you? You were a very strong and faithful Muslim."

"Nothing bad happened to me," I said. I barely recognized my own voice—it sounded weak and scared, with an unfamiliar tremor to it. "I am still a strong and faithful person," I said. My words were so quiet that someone outside shouted for me to speak up.

"Don't worry," Fatima said to me quietly before addressing the whole room. She looked like a lawyer addressing a jury. "But Zakhira, if you are still strong and faithful, then why am I hearing something strange being said about you?"

Clever, I thought. If she forced me to reveal with my own lips that I was no longer a Muslim, the crowd would turn against me. I tried to push back, telling her I didn't know what she'd heard about me. But again my voice was almost inaudible.

Fatima took a step closer and held her arms out wide, palms up. Her voice had a tone of sorrow in it, as if she were a survivor trying to reason with a former attacker. "You were an active volunteer in a well-known Islamic organization. You were born into a strong, faithful Muslim family. You served the orphans and lived well. I can't imagine why you'd become a Christian."

The answer came out of my mouth too quickly for me to think it through. "I read the Qur'an and became a Christian."

"What?" Fatima shot back, her calm, reasonable act vanishing in an instant. "I've read the Qur'an many times, just like all the people in this room. But none of us have become a kafir like you." The room swelled with approval, a few of the men shouting out "Kafir!" in agreement. Fatima paused and picked up a copy of the Qur'an from a table and held it triumphantly above her head. "The Qur'an is a book of Allah. It's a complete book, covering every aspect of life. It alone has the power to change lives, and whoever reads it can't be led astray. Instead they will find themselves set upon the right path. I am wondering: Have you really read the Qur'an? Surely everyone here knows that if a kafir reads this book, they will come back to Islam."

The applause lasted almost a full minute. The longer it went on, the angrier I became. How could she say that the Qur'an was the only book that could bring change? Everything I had read told me that the Qur'an is not the Word of God. Instead, it is a confused, misleading work that mullahs deliberately try to stop Muslims from studying too closely.

I checked my anger and took a breath. "If the Qur'an really does show the right way, as you say, I have some questions for you." Fatima nodded, and I felt my confidence rise as I went on. "If you will give satisfactory answers to all of my questions, then I promise I will come back to Islam without any hesitation at all. But if you're unable to answer even a single one of my questions fully, then I want you to promise in front of all these people that you will accept a gift from me."

"Of course," she said. "What questions do you have?"

"Well, you say that the Qur'an is a complete book and that it has all the details in it we could ever need. That's what you said, right?"

"It is."

"I would like to look at it then. Obviously, being an unclean kafir, I can't touch the Qur'an, so I'll need you to read it for me."

She agreed, opened the book to the verse I indicated, and read loudly enough for everyone in the room to hear: "And this Qur'an is not such as could ever be invented in despite of Allah; but it is a confirmation of that which was before it and an exposition of that which is decreed for mankind—Therein is no doubt—from the Lord of the Worlds."[15]

I gave her another reference to turn to, and again she read aloud: "We reveal the Scripture unto thee as an exposition of all things, and a guidance and a mercy and good things for those who have surrendered (to Allah)."[16]

"Thank you," I said. "I just want to ask: Are you sure this book is the exposition of all things?"

"Of course I am. Didn't you understand what I just read?"

"I understood, but I want to know that you are 100 percent sure of what you read."

"Yes, 100 percent sure."

"Okay," I said. "Then can you please tell me how many prophets or messengers have been sent by Allah?"

She couldn't hide the derision from her voice. "You became Christian because of this easy question? According to Islam, there are 124,000 prophets and messengers who came from Allah."

I ignored the murmurs and laughter rippling through the room and pressed on. "Can you please show me in the Qur'an all the names of the prophets and messengers? You don't need to tell me everything about each of the 124,000—just their names will do."

She froze. Like all Muslims, she believed in the 124,000 prophets sent by Allah. But unlike most of them, she knew that neither the Qur'an nor the hadith made that declaration. The 124,000 was just something Muslims believed, even though it wasn't in any of their holy books.

She was trapped. Either she admitted that the Qur'an was not the definitive source of all information, or she denounced a core belief that every Muslim assumed was right.

I smiled at her, remembering how stunned I had felt when John had opened my eyes to all this. "If you want, you can use the Qur'an and read the names. I don't mind if you read from the hadith as well. We all know that without the hadith, the story of Islam isn't complete."

Fatima kept quiet. A heavy silence fell on the room.

"Please, I think you should answer soon, Fatima. Everyone is waiting for you."

Eventually she spoke. "I will come back another day and give you the answer. Now ask me your next question."

"No," I said. "You need to answer my first question, and then we'll move on to the next one."

"It's a big figure. I can't remember all those names by heart."

"Really?" I said. "Then what kind of cleric are you if can't find the names of all the prophets in the Qur'an or the hadith? Don't you know your way around those books?"

"Give me some time." Her voice was as hard as steel. "Then I'll bring the names to you."

The room shifted uncomfortably. "Okay," I said. "I'd like you to read a verse from the Qur'an, please. Make sure it's nice and loud so everybody can hear you." I gave her the reference, and once she found it, she started reading.

"Please," I interrupted, "not in Arabic. I'm not sure everybody here will understand it. Please read the Urdu translation."

Fatima cleared her throat and started again. "And We bestowed on him Isaac and Jacob, and We established the prophethood and the Scripture among his seed, and We gave him his reward in the world, and lo! in the Hereafter he verily is among the righteous."[17]

"Thank you. Tell me, according to this verse, from which ancestor does Hazrat Muhammad come?"

"From Hazrat Abraham."

"But the verse doesn't mention Hazrat Abraham."

"I know, but Hazrat Abraham had two sons, Hazrat Isaac and Hazrat Ishmael."

"Okay, and which son was an ancestor of the Prophet?"

"Hazrat Ishmael."

"So can you read that verse again, please? Really loudly this time so we can really understand what it says."

"We bestowed on him Isaac and Jacob, and We established the prophethood and the Scripture among his seed, and We gave him his reward in the world."

I paused awhile. "I'm confused, Fatima. As you just read, the Qur'an confirms that all the prophets and all the books come from the seed of Isaac and Jacob only. There is no mention of Hazrat Ishmael. Did Allah not have a plan for him and his descendants? And if the Qur'an is correct, and Hazrat Muhammad really does come from Hazrat Isaac or from Hazrat Jacob, doesn't that mean that Hazrat Muhammad came from the Jews?"

Now it was Fatima's voice that faltered. "No, he's not from Hazrat Isaac or Hazrat Jacob. He's from Hazrat Ishmael."

"But that's not what the Qur'an says here. Why aren't you accepting what it says? It seems to me as though you're denying it. I'm the kafir, but even I agree with the Qur'an on this: all the prophets and all the scriptures really do come from the seeds of Isaac and Jacob, as both the Qur'an and the Holy Bible say."

She thought for a moment before trying to strike back. "Are you saying it's too difficult for Allah to raise a prophet from a nation other than the Jews? Are you saying Allah isn't strong enough? That would be blasphemous, Zakhira."

A thunder of claps filled the room, forcing me to wait before I could speak again. "Fatima, it is written seven times in the Qur'an that Allah never changes his words or decisions." I listed all the references and, just like before, had her read them in Urdu, loud enough for everyone to hear.

When she finished, I stood up for the first time in the meeting. "It is you who are guilty of blasphemy, not me. You are the one denying the Qur'an, not me. Why can't you say that the Qur'an is right in this matter?"

As I said this, people in the room started shouting at Fatima.

"Shut up!"

"Don't deny the Qur'an!"

"The girl is right. She's accepting what it says, but you're denying it."

Fatima sat down and waved me away. "I don't want to continue this talk. My thoughts are a little hazy today. I would rather come back again when I feel better and have been able to prepare. Then we will talk further."

I smiled at her. "That's fine. But you have to take the gift I promised you." I hurried out of the room, pulled my Holy Bible from the corner in the kitchen where I'd hidden it, and returned to my spot.

I held the book high above my head, just as she had done with the Qur'an when the meeting started. "This is the living Word of God. It has removed all my hazy thinking, and I believe it will clear your mind too."

I held it out to her. "Take it."

She stared at it, her hands locked in her lap. She had no idea how powerful the book was or how much it had changed my life. It felt strange that I was about to give away the book I'd fought so hard to gain. It was my only copy of the Holy Bible, but if I could save one life by giving it away, that would be a wonderful result. Besides, I was going to die soon anyway, and if I hadn't given it away by then, it would certainly be destroyed once I was killed.

"You made a promise," I said. "And you really shouldn't be afraid of a book that's mentioned in the oath all Muslims say daily. What you should be afraid of is denying what God has written. If you do that, you are no longer a Muslim."

The whole room was looking at Fatima.

She waited, then slowly reached out her hand. Her trembling fingers closed around the black leather cover.

†

Chaos erupted in the room as soon as Fatima left. People pressed around me, and I felt the heat of their breath as they shouted and pushed and pulled, arguing among themselves about what had just happened.

I could sense the commotion around me, but I wasn't part of it. I was thanking my God for the way my eyes had been drawn to the Qur'an earlier that morning, leading me to wonder about Abraham, Isaac, and Ishmael.

I was thanking my God for removing all the dust from my brain.

And I was thanking him that when the moment came for me to die—perhaps tomorrow, perhaps in a week or two— I could trust that the power of the Holy Spirit would be just as present as it had been that morning.

When I agreed to die in jihad, my aim was to kill as many people as possible through my own death. Now, as a Christian martyr, my death would mark the point that many people started to search for new life in God. I had never been more sure of anything in my life.

20

I fell to my knees at the side of my bed and thanked God for the way the debate had unfolded. Most clerics would have dismissed my question about the 124,000 prophets out of hand, but to my surprise, it had left Fatima with nothing to say. Only God could have caused her to get so easily confused, just as only God could have given me the words to say.

Though it hadn't been my intention, I realized I had used the same techniques with Fatima that I'd been taught at the madrassa. I had been polite and friendly, offering to get her a glass of water, and then I placed a doubt in her mind—as well as the minds of those watching—over the names of all those prophets. The deeper our conversation went, the clearer it became that her assumptions were based on weak foundations.

I hadn't planned any of it, and part of me had been surprised to hear myself speak the way I had to Fatima. But I was grateful to God all the same, even for the way he was able to redeem my time in the madrassa and use it to shine a light of truth.

I can't count all the times I'd been told how to bring a Christian into Islam. I had been taught to ask how it was possible for God to have a son, since that would require God to have a wife. The Trinity was another area I was told to target. How could three Gods ever live in harmony with each other? Finally, I was instructed to argue that the Christian Bible has been corrupted from its original form, with all traces of the life of Muhammad removed.

These arguments were never backed up with sound logic or proof, but that did not seem to matter. The strategy for converting a Christian rested on one key aim: to sow as many seeds of doubt as possible in a believer's mind.

After the first debate, I decided to use the same strategy in arguing against Islam, regardless of how many days I had left to live.

After watching Fatima grow tongue-tied and seeing the people get angry at her, it now seemed even less likely that I would be allowed to live a whole month. But I knew that no matter how many debates I faced, I could approach them with confidence and courage. Islam was full of holes, and God had my back. I had never been more certain of anything in my life.

I trust you completely, God, I vowed in my bedroom later that night. *I will shout the truth about you and about Islam as loudly as I possibly can.*

†

When I walked into the meeting room the next day, I held tightly to the Scripture I'd been reciting in my head: "When you are brought before synagogues, rulers and authorities, do not worry about how you will defend yourselves or what you will say, for the Holy Spirit will teach you at that time what you should say."[18]

Even though the passage was one of my favorites, it hit me with all the force of a hurricane when it came to my mind in the early-morning light. It banished any traces of anxiety and filled me with the knowledge that I was right where God wanted me to be.

A few hours later I watched the cleric arrive. He was a heavyset gentleman, probably younger than my father, but with an air that suggested he thought he was the wisest man who had ever walked the earth. People scuttled out of his way as he swept in. With his brow furrowed in mock concentration, he nodded at the men in the room with the longest beards.

Even before he reached the front, he threw his arms out wide and started speaking. "My dear, my beloved daughter." He looked at me briefly before turning to face the rest of the room. "You were blessed to be born into Islam. Did you know that Hazrat Jesus wished to be born a Muslim like you? The Christians who live among us are so unworthy and poor that some of them are working to clean our roads. Christians are the sweepers, the ones who carry out the lower-level jobs that no true Muslim would ever want. Why would you want to join them?"

He held up his hand and nodded at the murmurs of approval.

"Sir," I said, "I'm glad you're here, and I hope you can answer a question that has been troubling me for some time. Why are there so many Muslims standing on street corners throughout the city, begging for money or food? And why do they always say, 'Give to me in the name of Allah' or 'Give to me in the name of Muhammad'?"

"My daughter, on the day of judgment, there will be no

flesh on the skin of those beggars. It is written in the hadith that Allah will not give a single look to those people. He will hate them and will turn his face from them."[19]

"You are absolutely right. I, too, have read that hadith. But it is also written that no one earns his food better than the one who works with his hands, like David the prophet of Allah. Do you know that hadith? It's reported by al-Bukhari and others. I can find it for you if you like."

He stood in silence, his face frozen.

"Let me show you the reference," I said, reaching for the hadith I had brought with me.

"Yes, yes!" He was unable to keep the frustration from his voice. "There's no need to read it out loud. It is written as you say."

"Then surely that means that the Christians who work with their own hands are blessed, correct? They choose not to beg, but to clean and sweep. According to these texts, they are the ones who will be so close to Allah that there is no gap between them. According to what you have shown us, these Christians, though they are poor, will be the ones Allah will want to look at, not the Muslim beggars you say he will despise. So tell me, isn't it the Christian poor who are blessed rather than the Muslims?"

Again, the cleric was mute. All his bravado and arrogance had evaporated. But I was not finished. "There's one more thing I want to ask," I said. "You claimed that Jesus wished to be born into a Muslim nation. Did you know that the Qur'an says Jesus ascended to heaven alive?[20] It explains that he will come back again at the end of days. So without his return to the earth, there will be no end—no day of judgment. Isn't that right?"

"Yes."

"So that means Hazrat Muhammad can't come out of his grave until Jesus Christ returns. Only Jesus Christ has the authority to call the dead from the grave and make them alive, for only Jesus Christ has done these miracles on this earth. Even the Qur'an confirms this. Is there any place in the Qur'an that shows that Hazrat Muhammad performed any miracles at all?"

The cleric had been looking at the ground for some time. Without raising his eyes, he got up and walked toward the door. The whole room watched in silence as he left, shoulders slumped and head hung low. "Someone led her astray very badly," he announced as he paused at the door. "Now it's going to be very difficult to bring her back to Islam."

†

When my mother came to see me in my room that night, she was so happy. She giggled like a schoolgirl as we talked about the mullah and the contrast between his elaborate entrance and his humble departure.

I was still smiling as I closed my eyes and let myself drift into sleep.

In my dreams that night, I saw a ditch that was as real as any I'd ever seen in person. I stood in the middle of it, my feet half covered in stagnant water. To my right was beauty like I had never witnessed. The land was full of lush grass and gently rolling hills. To my left, the view could not have been more different. The land was dry, the earth was cracked, and the sun had long since scorched all life from the place.

I became aware that all my family members who were still living at home were on the left of the ditch. One by one, I reached out for them, grabbing my mother's hand first and guiding her over to the right. Next my brother crossed over, then my little sister. At last I held out my hand for my father, but he would not reach toward me. There was no way I could stretch far enough to reach him.

When I woke the next morning, the dream was still alive within me. I knew what it meant, and I knew what I had to do. I needed to act fast—to pray and then share my faith with my brother and younger sister.

Later that day, when my father was out of the house, I asked them to come to the kitchen with me and my mother.

"I don't know what's going to happen to me," I said. "I don't know whether I'll live to see the end of this week or the end of the month, but I have to tell you that everything I'm saying in these debates is the truth. You must remember—Jesus is the only one who can save you."

They both sat and stared. Neither of them had ever been as devout a Muslim as I had once been, but this was still a risk. My mouth felt dry as I broke the silence.

"You can see that these scholars don't have any answers. They don't know what they're talking about. And you can tell they're scared of having Christians reveal the truth to others. Why would they want to kill me if I weren't a threat? Why are they worried about me talking about my faith in Christ? It's because they know that Islam is not right and that Christianity is."

"She's right," my mother said. "I'm a Christian too."

They looked at each other, eyes wide and full of tears.

†

On the fourth day of my house arrest, Fatima returned. The room was just as full for the third debate as it had been for the first. But this time she was prepared.

"I was unwell last time," she said. "Today I'm feeling much

better, and I have a question I'd like you to answer." She held the Holy Bible I had given her over her head. "Is this the book that changed the way you saw Islam?"

"Yes."

"And do you still claim that this book is the truth as revealed by God?"

"Yes."

Turning to everyone in the room, she said, "We all know that the prophets and angels are so good, wise, and pure that they never made mistakes. But this book claims that men like Lot and David were sinners."

The chorus of approval that followed Fatima's words was so loud I had to shout. "I learned from my family while I was still a Muslim that everyone makes mistakes, even the mullahs. The wisest people are the ones who make mistakes and learn from them."

"You're wrong. This is just something people say to children. It has no truth in Islam. The prophets never commit sin. If they ever do make a mistake, it's only a tiny one, and it's not a sin."

"Really?" I said. "You think they never commit any sin? Since we're here, I have some questions about Islam. Maybe you can help me. Tell me this first: Who is Adam?"

"He's the first prophet in Islam, the first prophet on the earth from Allah."

"Okay. Can you tell me why he came from heaven to earth?"

"The Qur'an tells us that it's because he ate the fruit Allah said was forbidden. Some texts say it was an apple; some say it was wheat."

"He ate what Allah had forbidden. Does that mean he disobeyed?"

"Yes."

"When we disobey, it's called sin. God said, 'Do not commit adultery,' and when we do, it's a sin. Whenever we go against God's Word and do the things he tells us not to do, we're guilty of sin. So if the first prophet disobeyed God and sinned, how can you say the others didn't sin?"

"What Adam did wasn't sin," Fatima retorted. "It was just disobedience."

"So what if a prophet had stolen something? Would that be okay? Shouldn't he have his hands cut off in punishment?"

Fatima shrugged and sat down. I kept going, turning to the whole room. "This is the truth of the Holy Bible: it never hides the sin of a person or a prophet. It tells us that we all are weak and that God still chooses to use us. Nothing is hidden from him."

Just as he had during the previous two debates, my father sat along the wall near the door, as far away from me as he could possibly get. Fatima looked at him and said, "I tell you, she is not coming back. Not ever."

Gathering up her possessions, including the Holy Bible, she turned to leave. When she reached my father, she stopped. "I don't want to talk to her anymore."

21

After Fatima and the overconfident cleric walked out of their debates, a string of others followed. They all arrived with their arguments mapped out and their lines scripted. Having given away my copy of the Holy Bible, I spent hours each day studying the Qur'an and various hadiths, as well as browsing the books my father owned.

The fourth debate was with a local cleric who was the exact opposite of the previous two. From the start, he was nervous and quiet, and he never once looked in my direction. Instead, he stood at the front of the room and read from his notes as if this were a lecture.

"This book, which she refers to as the Holy Bible, is not worthy to be read among females. I would ask all of you here—sisters, brothers, mothers, and fathers—to listen to these words written therein."

I recognized the passage immediately. It was the part in

Genesis that describes Lot's two daughters getting him drunk and sleeping with him. My mind scrambled to think of a response, but the cleric didn't pause.

"Would any of you want to read such writings among your family? Or what of Hazrat David? Listen to what happened when he was walking on his palace roof one day."

Hearing Scripture read aloud was like feeling the sun on a cold winter day. It filled me with life, and I could feel the hairs on the back of my neck stand up. Even though the cleric was trying to trick me, I wanted to thank him for bringing the Holy Bible with him and for reading it in front of all these people. Was it too much to hope that some of them might be feeling what I felt?

When the cleric had finished the story of David and Bathsheba, I stood up to speak. "We can read this Holy Bible among everyone, because it always tells the truth. It never lies. The Holy Bible makes it clear that Lot didn't know what his daughters were doing and that God was angry with them for their shameful act. And David's sin isn't hidden from us any more than it was hidden from God. What David did in secrecy, God revealed in the Holy Bible to let us know that he is watching over us all the time, whether we are kings, prophets, or ordinary people. God knows everything we do in secret, so we should fear God and remember that we human beings are sinners. None of us is perfect. Only God Almighty is the one who is both righteous and perfect."

I asked the cleric to wait a moment while I took one of my father's books down from the shelf. I opened it to a page I'd seen the previous day. "Would you read this out loud, please?" I handed him a book called *Beautiful Scenes in Heaven* by an Islamic scholar.

He looked at the book, then back at me.

"You'll need to translate it so everybody here can under-stand," I said.

"I don't want to read it." He closed the book and handed it back to me.

"You're feeling ashamed to read it in front of everyone here, aren't you? The writing is so explicit that I think even a mar-ried couple would feel embarrassed to read it together."

He shuffled his feet awhile and then folded his paper. "Perhaps we should continue this debate over e-mail."

I gave him my address, knowing that he would never make contact. And even if he did, I knew that God would pro-vide the words I needed, just as he had done in every debate. Though I was surrounded by people who wanted me dead, I sensed God's love and presence in ways I had never before experienced. He was closer than the air I breathed. Any fear I felt about how things might turn out, any nervousness about what arguments I would face, failed to have much of a hold on me. God's love was by far the brightest star in my universe.

†

The next debate took yet another direction. While the first four had been filled with spectators, this one was held late at night and only a handful of people were in the room. It did not take long for me to realize that this was not by accident.

"My daughter," the old cleric began. "You were blessed because you were born into a Muslim family. It's a great privi-lege to be in a Muslim family." He stopped, smiled widely, and lowered his voice to a whisper. "My daughter, if Christians have offered you money, please let us know. How much have they agreed to pay you? Whatever it is, we will give you more than they will, as long as you turn your back on their religion."

I was shocked. "You think that by offering me money I will

come back into darkness? What you're suggesting is as ridiculous as asking someone traveling in an airplane how much they would want to continue their journey by donkey. I'm an educated, sound-minded, healthy girl. If I needed money, I could go out and work for it. Why would I take a bribe and end up in all this trouble if I could be bought so easily?

"And there's one other thing for you to know. Whatever money you have belongs to my God. He is my Father; he alone is the Creator of the universe. Everything is under his control. According to the Holy Bible, he has numbered all the hairs on my head,[21] and he has sketched me on the palm of his hand.[22] He knows what I need, and he provides for me perfectly. Whenever I'm in need, I will call on him for help. I can give you his number if you like—it's 33:3. Whenever you need help, look up Jeremiah 33:3 and call out to God. He will answer you."

The cleric stared at me, his face set in stone. He turned back and whispered to some of the other men gathered around him.

"You are a young girl," he said, a half smile resting on his lips. "We can understand how these things happen. Maybe you fell in love with someone who is a Christian. Don't worry if you have. Just tell us who he is, and we'll bring him into Islam. Then the two of you can be married."

"You're right," I said. "I am in love. But not with any Christian boy I've met. I'm in love with Jesus Christ. Let him be in my life forever and ever. I'm not interested in anyone else."

He left soon after that. Just like the others, he delivered his verdict to my parents, telling them that I was crazy and that bringing me back into Islam would be nearly impossible.

†

The room was full again, and I was excited about the prospect of comparing the Word of God with the Qur'an in front of so many people.

"Today I'm going to talk from this book she loves so much," shouted a new cleric I had not seen before.

"Why?" I asked. "You don't believe that this is the Book of God. You clerics all say that it has been changed. We should talk from the Qur'an instead."

"No." He was facing the crowd, his back to me. He must have been making faces, for a ripple of laughter skimmed the room. "I've heard about the way you treat the Qur'an. Today I'm talking from the Bible. Have you read it?"

"Yes."

"Then why are you scared?"

"I'm not," I shot back, a little too quickly. More laughter. "I'm ready."

"Good." The cleric opened to Luke 3:16 with a flourish. "It is written here that Jesus said, 'One who is more powerful than I will come, the straps of whose sandals I am not worthy to untie.' Who else could Jesus be talking about but the Prophet Muhammad, peace be upon him."

I could not believe it. Was this really his best attempt at creating doubt in my mind?

"Okay," I said. "I've read this Holy Bible, and I think I know it better than you do, so let me explain." I reached over and took the book from his hand, my heart racing as I touched it. "You didn't read the whole passage, so you got confused about who was speaking. It wasn't Jesus who said that but John the Baptist, speaking *about* Jesus. Was Jesus even there at the time? Was Muhammad?"

Silence.

"Neither was. John was talking to the religious leaders. And look here." I pointed to the end of the verse he had read. "John says that the one who is coming next will baptize with fire, not water. Does the Qur'an have anything to say about people being baptized by fire?"

He said nothing.

"There are lots of verses about God sending someone great, but none of them refer to Muhammad. Like this one here," I said, flipping back to Deuteronomy 18:15: "Moses said to the Israelites, 'The LORD your God will raise up for you a prophet like me from among you, from your fellow Israelites. You must listen to him.' If you want to claim that this refers to Muhammad, then you would have to believe that Muhammad is from the brethren of Israel. You would have to believe that Muhammad was a Jew. I don't think these people would like it if you said that."

The laughter that had filled the room minutes earlier was a vague memory. In its place was only angry shouting. I had said all that I needed to, and I could feel the atmosphere sour. I slipped out as quickly as I could.

✝

The next day a new mullah came, holding copies of the Holy Bible, the Qur'an, and a set of scales. He placed the Qur'an on one side of the scales and the Holy Bible on the other. Then he went into the stance of a prizefighter—arms aloft, a satisfied smile beaming across his face. "See?" he said when the cheering in the room died down. "The Qur'an is heavier than the Bible. The Qur'an is from Allah. It's full of more truth than your so-called holy book."

He spun around to more cheering and cries of "Allahu Akbar!"

When the crowd quieted down a little, I shouted, "Sir, your scale is telling the truth! What belongs to God—the Holy Bible—is pointing up, and what belongs to the earth—the Qur'an—is pointing down."

My argument was as foolish as his, and my voice was lost among the shouting. In time the crowd fell silent, their eyes fixed on the grinning cleric, who apparently had no more points to make.

After the debate was over, one of the women from the neighborhood came up to me. Through the slit in her veil, I could see her eyes popping with rage. "You should be ashamed for bringing disgrace on your father!"

My mother stood at my side, silent while the woman unleashed a steady flow of insults.

When she finally finished, I was able to talk. "Auntie," I said, hoping the term of respect would calm her a little. "These people are coming to debate me. I'm open to talking with every one of them, but none of them are giving me any answers. If they could, I'd return to Islam right now. But none of them have anything noteworthy to say. They are spiritually blind. Even those who have read the Holy Bible only skimmed it for lines they could use against me. But when you study both the Holy Bible and the Qur'an, as I have, you'll see that Islam doesn't make sense anymore."

She turned to my mother, waving her hand in my face. "This is all because she studied and went too deep. That's why she is rebelling against Islam."

"Yes," I said as she left. "You are exactly right."

†

That night my mother was full of hope as we met to talk and pray in my room. "Perhaps they'll change their minds," she said.

I looked at my mother and tried to summon a smile.

"You're saying things that are making people think," she said. "You're asking questions they've never had to ask before and forcing them to think deeply about Islam. Maybe if the debates carry on like this, they'll understand too. And maybe they won't kill you after all."

I agreed with everything she said about the debates, just not her final conclusion. The longer this went on and the greater fools the clerics made of themselves, the more likely it seemed that my death was not just inevitable. It was imminent.

22

"Open this Bible and read from Genesis."

It had been some time since I had last seen my college lecturer. Now she was here, holding out the Holy Bible to me. I had always been a diligent student, never handing in an assignment late or showing up to class without being fully prepared. I had never disobeyed any of my teachers, particularly this one.

Miss Shah was the best teacher I'd ever had. She was a scientist with a keen mind and a fierce belief in the value of education. She was twenty years older than I was but still single. I had spent hours wondering what battles she must have fought to get to where she was.

It was not hard to remember back to when I believed Miss Shah and my other teachers held the key to my future. Even when I was living as a secret believer, I valued education highly. I trusted my lecturers at college to guide me toward my goal of getting a degree and a job, and the freedom those opportunities would bring. I had thanked God for those teachers many times.

But something within me shifted the moment I saw Miss Shah standing in the meeting room. I realized that she was no longer on my side.

I held out my hand and felt the familiar weight of the Holy Bible.

"Chapter 1, verses 11 and 12 please, Zakhira."

I did as I was told and started reading the Creation account, where God told the land to produce vegetation.

"Louder," Miss Shah said. "So everyone can hear."

When I finished, she had me read later in the chapter, where God created the sun, moon, and stars.

"Tell me, according to science, what should be created first: vegetation or sunlight?"

I knew instantly where she was heading. "Sunlight, then vegetation."

"Yes, and since we know that Allah can't make a single mistake, when we read here that he created vegetation first and the sun second, the Bible itself must be in error. And if these first pages of the book are false, then everything that follows must be questioned as well."

She had me. After a week of debates with clerics whose arguments had slowly turned to dust, Miss Shah had beaten me within a few minutes. I looked down at the Holy Bible, fought back tears, and begged God for help.

"Miss," I said a moment later, my blood pulsing and my eyes clear. "God isn't wrong, nor is the Holy Bible false. God made everything according to science because he is the Creator and source of all, including science."

I read the entire account of Creation. "Miss, is it clear to you yet? God created light first in verse 3, and then he created vegetation in verse 11. And just as an indoor plant can survive without direct sunlight, so the earth was able to grow before the sun was formed."

She looked unimpressed.

"My daughter." She brushed the air aside with a sweep of her hand. "Perhaps the Christians didn't tell you this, but they're actually following three Gods. They call them the Trinity, but their logic isn't sound. We believe Allah is mighty enough on his own."

"You're wrong," I said, feeling the looks of disapproval around me. "Christians also believe in one God, but he has shown himself in three different ways. In Moses' time, he showed himself in fire. At the time of the last prophet of the Holy Bible, John the Baptist, God revealed himself in a human body as Jesus Christ."

She looked skeptical.

"You can see for yourself in the Qur'an," I went on. "It's written in Surah 21, verse 91, and Surah 66, verse 12."

I was not surprised that she wanted to talk about the Trinity. Like many Muslims, I had been taught that Christianity has three major flaws: it follows three Gods; it claims that Jesus is the Son of God; and its book, the Bible, has been changed. Most Muslims accept these criticisms without really trying to find the truth for themselves.

As Miss Shah seemed to have little else to say, I decided to press on with my defense of the Trinity.

"Why does the Qur'an refer to Allah using the word *we* 1,297 times, the word *our* 217 times, and the word *us* 88 times? Shouldn't it be *I* if he is as you say?"

The room filled with murmurs again.

"If the Christians are so wrong about this, why does the Qur'an tell Christians and Jews they have nothing to fear?"

More murmurs.

"Lo!" I recited from the Qur'an, "those who believe, and those who are Jews, and Sabeans, and Christians—Whosoever believeth in Allah and the Last Day and doeth right—there shall no fear come upon them neither shall they grieve."[23]

The room fell silent. Miss Shah left. The debate was over.

†

It was inevitable that one day I turned up in the meeting room to find my uncle standing at the front, waiting to debate me. He was my father's brother, the same one who had found out about my writing to the Bible Society. The same one who had led the first calls for me to be killed on the street.

From the start of the debate, he was shouting, accusing me of being a kafir and disrespecting the prophet Muhammad. I could feel the anger rising within me, but I tried to remain calm.

When he paused to take a breath, I seized the opportunity. "Tell me, when Hazrat Muhammad was twenty-five years old and he married his first wife, Khadijah, who performed the marriage ceremony? And was it a Jewish ceremony or a Hindu ceremony?"

"You foolish girl," he sniffed. "Khadijah accepted Islam."

"But there was no Islam until fifteen years later, when Hazrat Muhammad was forty years old. So did Muhammad become a Jew? And if he did, why do Muslims hate Jews so much today?"

It was a dangerous thing to say, and it sent my uncle into an even greater rage. He put his face right up next to mine, and I saw that his eyes were wild and his cheeks were flushed beneath his beard. "You've been led astray, my daughter. They've brainwashed you!"

"No, Uncle." I was a little surprised at how calm my voice sounded. "They haven't. I've just discovered the truth."

"The truth? Everybody knows that the Bible has been changed. There's an original manuscript in Egypt that has the story of Hazrat Muhammad in it."

"Uncle," I said with a laugh, "I will pay your travel expenses if you go there and bring home a copy to compare with the Holy Bible I've been reading. If the Egyptian Bible is different from the one I've read, I promise I will come back to Islam. But if they're the same, you have to become a Christian like me."

He threw up his hands and spun on his heels, muttering about how I was impossible to help.

†

I tried to find a pattern, but it seemed that the people brought in to debate me were selected at random. Even if I refuted a series of outrageous claims about the Bible one day, a few days later I might face a different cleric who asked exactly the same questions. These attacks seemed as uncoordinated and confused as the Qur'an itself.

In the third week of my house arrest, I received another visit from a lecturer at my old college. This woman had occasionally taught me chemistry. "I heard that you'd been led astray, and I felt so bad," she said to me as we waited for my father to show the rest of the people in. "What happened to you?"

"Nothing bad happened, Miss. I'm very well."

"It's really sad to change your religion. How was it possible for anyone to take you from the right path?"

"I don't think anyone could take me away from this path I'm on now," I said. "And I wouldn't want them to either. This is the path that leads to eternal life."

"You know, I studied in the UK and America, but nothing could change my faith in Islam."

"I'm sorry that you went all that way but still came home thirsty. Without the living water, nothing can satisfy you."

She mumbled that she wasn't thirsty for what I was describing and turned away. I felt bold and free, so I leaned in close. "You have no desire to seek the Lord, no thirst for eternal life. So you need to pray to Jesus Christ and ask him to make you hungry and thirsty for him. Only when you do that will you see the Lord."

She stood up and spoke so loudly that the whole room fell silent. "I didn't come here to listen to you. I came here to tell you what's important."

"Miss, if you won't listen to me, then how will you know why I left Islam? Isn't that why you're here?"

I did not expect her to soften, but she did. "Okay, tell me what made you change your religion."

"I will. But first, may I ask you something about chemistry?"

"Are you joking?"

"No, Miss, I'm serious. I just have a question that I want to ask now so I won't forget it later. But if you aren't willing, that's okay."

She waved her hand, so I carried on. "If you are asked in an exam to explain how to prepare a certain gas, what's the best answer?"

"Start with the heading, then list the apparatus, then the procedure, and lastly the precautions. That's it."

"That's helpful—thank you, Miss. How did you get to be so good at chemistry?"

"Allah gave me the gift." She was unable to hide the smile from her voice.

"So imagine I'm in the exam, and I write my heading:

'Preparation of Oxygen.' Then I write, 'Potatoes are so nice,' then 'My mother and I went shopping,' then 'My baby sister is crying,' and finally 'That's how you make oxygen.' What kind of marks would I get?"

"None. You clearly wouldn't know anything about oxygen."

"Tell me about Allah. How much wiser than us is he?"

"Unlimited," she said. "He is the source of all wisdom."

"So why did Allah not show his wisdom when he was inspiring the writing of the Qur'an?"

"You're wrong," she said. "Perhaps you didn't read the Qur'an correctly."

"That's possible. Could we read something from it together now? I've always liked the story of Jonah."

I had her open the Qur'an to Surah 10, the chapter titled "Yunus" (Jonah), and listened while she read. When she was done, I asked her a simple question: "What did you learn about Jonah from what you just read?"

She stayed silent.

"Shouldn't a passage with the heading 'Jonah' contain at least some information about the prophet? But in all those 109 verses you just read, there was only one that even mentioned his name. Why can't Allah, who has higher wisdom than you, accurately tell the story in the Qur'an?"

She had nothing to say. Nor did anyone else in the room.

"If you look at the Holy Bible, you'll see that everything is clear. Genesis means 'beginning,' and that's exactly what the book describes. Exodus refers to a situation where many people leave a place at the same time, and in it you can read all about the Israelites leaving Egypt. If you want to read about Jonah, just look at the book called Jonah. It's the same with Jeremiah and other prophets. This is the holy book of God, and we can see his wisdom clearly through it. The Qur'an, on the other hand, is confusing and misleading."

My former teacher sat in silence, as did everybody else in the room. Since no one made a move to stop me, I went on. "There are other reasons why I accepted Christianity. Like the fact that Jesus Christ taught love. He told people, 'Love your enemies' and 'If anyone slaps you on the right cheek, turn to them the other cheek also.' But all Islam ever taught me was hate. It says in Surah Muhammad 47:4 to kill those who never embrace Islam."

I was about to start a new point when she stood up, leaned in close, and whispered, "I really don't know what to say."

I looked at her carefully. Her eyes were honest. She looked like she was close to tears.

"Then I have good news for you. Jesus Christ loves you. That's the reason you're here today. He wants to reveal the truth to you. He wants you to know him."

I watched her eyes flick from me to the roomful of skeptical men. When she looked back at me, her face was creased with worry. "I have to go. I have a class to teach."

†

Later that evening, I poured out my thanks to God. I prayed for my teacher, that her spiritual eyes might be opened. I prayed the same thing for my father, my brother, and my sisters. I prayed for myself, that my heart and mind would be ready for whatever the next day would bring.

As I prayed, it hit me that there was a pattern to these debates after all. But it had little to do with the agenda of the leaders of my religious community. The common factor was the way that God was using me.

At first I'd seen the debates as trials of my own belief and understanding of God, as if I were being judged not only by the clerics but by God himself. The longer the debates went on, however, the more I saw that God was using me as his mouthpiece, revealing his truth to those who needed to hear it.

It was a powerful realization, and I felt a burden slip from my shoulders.

These debates were a gift. From now on, I would receive them gladly.

23

My father had laughed when I first said it. It was not a small laugh either; it was a roar so loud all the traders in the market stopped their business and looked at us. He was clean shaven at the time, and he laughed so hard that the veins in his neck stood out. I liked the sound of his laugh, so I said it again.

"I want the ice cream shaped like a panda. That one right there."

As predicted, he laughed again, placing his hand on my shoulder. It was gentle and warm, and I wanted to reach up and hold it. I wanted to weave my tiny fingers around his, to hold on to this moment and never let it go.

"Why not something else?" His eyes sparkled as he teased me. "Look, they even have sliced cow's foot. I know how much you like that."

I made a face, crossed my arms, and pretended to be mad.

"Cows can be found anywhere, but pandas only live in China. That's why I want the ice cream."

My father gave in and then told me it was time to head back home. I walked beside him, holding the panda ice cream like a trophy, carefully licking up the drips and trying to make the treat last as long as possible.

It was my happiest moment with him.

In my memory, he started growing his beard soon after. The beard signaled an end to his placing his hand on my shoulder, an end to his filling the air with laughter, an end to my walking alone with him to the market.

The truth was less dramatic. The signs of physical affection, the sound of laughter, and those daddy-daughter moments were never regular features of my life. That memory stands in isolation, a single event in stark contrast to all the others. Even before he grew his beard, he was characteristically distant and cold.

As the debates continued and my father watched silently from the back, I knew he would never change his mind. There was no nostalgia for him, no idyllic period to return to. The moments of warmth were as temporary as the panda ice cream that had melted in the sun. As the third week of debates drew to a close, I decided two things needed to happen urgently.

I'd had little contact with my two older sisters since they married and moved out. That made me even more determined to share my faith with my brother and younger sister. I had met with them nightly since all this began. We would talk about what had been said in the debates, and they would ask questions about Christianity. It was important to me that, along with seeing the risks of becoming a Christian and the flaws of Islam, they knew about the wonderful freedom and truth of what it means to be a follower of Jesus.

One night, about three weeks into the debates, my brother and sister told me they were ready to give their lives to Jesus. With our voices hushed to make sure my father did not wake up, my mother and I sat with them in my room and led them in prayer.

When we had finished our tearstained embraces, I gave them a warning: "Be careful. Don't tell anyone you're a Christian yet. When the right time comes, you'll know it. But until then, you have to keep your new faith secret."

†

More debates took place in the days that followed, and as before, I tried to take any opportunity I could to share my faith. Sometimes that was harder than other times. The atmosphere in the room was beginning to shift. No longer was I facing educated, thoughtful lecturers from my college. Nor were there foolish clerics hoping to win me back by weighing the Qur'an and the Holy Bible side by side. Instead, my opponents were all pompous clerics who tried to patronize me.

Sometimes, when they felt threatened, they would get angry. It became increasingly common for me to find myself shouted at, called an infidel, and accused of blasphemy. At times like these, the conversation felt less like a debate and more like a rally to stir up hatred among the crowd.

At one such time, a mullah was shouting at me for not following Muhammad's sunna—the collection of his actions and deeds.

"Are *you* following all of his sunna?" I asked when his tirade paused.

"Of course!" He looked around at the people in the audience, many of whom were nodding at him.

"I don't think so," I said. "You're missing one."

"Which one?"

"Hazrat Muhammad was fifty-one years old when he married Hazrat Aisha, who was just six years old at the time, a few years younger than Hazrat Muhammad's daughter Fatimah. He waited three years, but still she was nine years old when he took her to his bed."

He looked at me blankly. I pressed on. "Do you have a daughter?"

"Yes."

"How old is she?"

"Eight."

"Tell me honestly: Wasn't Hazrat Aisha too young to be taken as a wife when she was still playing with dolls? According to this current era, it would be rape or child abuse."

He held up his hand. "Hazrat Muhammad just obeyed Allah."

"Really?" I knew that with every word, I was fueling the hatred of me in the room. "If Hazrat Muhammad was instructed by Allah to take a child as his wife, why did he refuse the first two caliphs of Islam, Abu Bakr Siddique and Umar Farooq, when they asked to marry his own daughter Fatimah? Why, instead of those old men, did Hazrat Muhammad choose for her husband Ali, who was about twenty-five years old? And why, when Hazrat Muhammad had multiple wives, did he never allow his son-in-law Ali to get a second wife, even though he desired to marry the daughter of Abu Jahal? Hazrat Muhammad allowed other followers to be polygamists, but he didn't want to upset his daughter Fatimah."

The mullah was quiet. He looked at me with nothing short of pure hatred. As the crowd started shouting, I made my final point. "I became a Christian because in the Holy

Bible, the law is the same for everyone. There is no hypocrisy within its pages."

†

Three days before the end of the fourth week, I had my twenty-first debate. Thanks to my opponent, the atmosphere in the room was different from the start. He was an imam, a famous cleric from the other side of the country. He'd drawn a large crowd—easily the biggest one yet. I guessed that between the people wedged together on the floor, those in the courtyard and the street outside, and the others gathered elsewhere in the house, there must have been almost two hundred in attendance.

The room was silent. I watched people strain to get a better look at my opponent, and I took a look too. I remembered seeing him on TV once or twice. I had never listened to what he was preaching, but it was obvious he was a celebrity in our community. For the first time in all the debates, I felt a shiver of nerves run through me.

"Tell me," he said as he got up to speak, "is it right to worship Jesus—to praise him or bow down to him? Does a prophet deserve that?"

My brain blanked. I had nothing to say. It was all I could do to look at the imam and not be paralyzed by the silence all around us. "That's—that's a good question," I stammered. "What do you think?"

His smile was gentle and genuine, and for a moment I wanted to trust him. I got a glimpse of how good it would feel to have all these people look at me with respect and awe rather than hatred and contempt.

"He was human," the imam said. "He was created by Allah, the exalted one. But it's Allah and Allah alone we should praise."

I looked around the room. For once, people were staring not at me but at my opponent. They were nodding along. But how many of them, I wondered, had ever read the Qur'an for themselves? How many of them had studied it or asked hard questions of their clerics instead of simply accepting surface-level answers? How many of them had gone deep and faced the confusion and lies at the heart of the Qur'an?

I felt so sorry for them. As I stood up to speak, my tongue was released. I called out some references in the Qur'an and asked the imam to read them. He did not argue. When he read three different accounts of Allah commanding the angels to bow down before Adam, the imam stared back at me, as calm as anything.

"Those three references all show Allah commanding the angels to bow down to a human. Is that right?"

"I don't know," he said, unperturbed.

"Might it be that this was a kind of practice for when Jesus was born? The Qur'an tells us that Jesus Christ is both God's Holy Spirit (Ruh al-Qudus) and his Word (Kalimatullah) in human flesh. Jesus Christ is more worthy of praise and worship than Adam. And aren't we allowed to worship God whether he is in the form of the Holy Spirit, whom no one can see, or as human flesh?"

The imam remained unfazed by my words. He simply sat and listened, concentrating on what I was saying as if I were defending Islam rather than exposing it. I told him about the 353 Old Testament prophecies that Jesus fulfilled and about how at Jesus' baptism God sent his Spirit in the form of a dove. Still the imam just stared politely at me.

Then he left. There was no shouting, no retaliation—just a quick exit as the crowd watched in silence.

A few moments later, the room exploded. People were

shouting, waving their arms, and surging like an angry tide. I sat down and thanked God for again providing me with knowledge and wisdom that was not mine. I blocked out the sounds of the room and poured out my gratitude to God.

When I looked up, there were no angry faces shouting at me. All I saw were people's backs as the last few shuffled quietly out of the room. Only one person was looking at me: my father. His stare was more cold and lifeless than I had ever seen it.

✝

I was grateful that my brother and sister had become Christians, but there was one other matter I had to attend to before my father brought the debates to a close. I sensed that my time was running short, and I knew I needed to act quickly.

My mother helped me, first by making sure the house was clear when I made the phone call and then by taking me to the market the next day. We said good-bye at the market near her workshop and agreed to meet each other there within two hours.

When I walked into John's lab again, it was as if the fatwa and the mobs and the debates had never happened. We talked easily about his work and my mother's conversion and my brother's healing. I could not stop smiling, rejoicing at what God was doing in both our lives.

But reality soon set in.

"We don't have long," he said. "My pastor is ready."

He led me out of his lab and into his car. Then we headed to the other side of the city, to a neighborhood I had never been to before. It was one of the poorest areas around and was home to many of the Christians who swept the streets.

In the past, I would have been nervous to be seen there.

Even after becoming a Christian, it was risky for someone dressed in a full Islamic veil like I was to be seen there. Not all Christians, I knew, were like John. In fact, many Christians in Pakistan were hostile toward Muslims. As a result of years of mistreatment and hostility, they sometimes reacted out of fear and mistrust.

But that day I was not scared at all. I knew there was a risk I might be stopped and questioned, but what could they do to me that was worse than what my father had in mind? We parked the car and walked the last few blocks to an unremarkable-looking building on an unimpressive street. I did not mind that people were staring at me: I was dressed as one of their persecutors. They had every right to be scared.

Everyone knew what Islamic extremists were doing to Christians. Not long before, a Christian girl who was charged with stealing had been given the death penalty by an Islamic court, and a Christian man whose crime wasn't even specified was hog-tied and dragged through the streets, again with the support of the Islamic officials. When the mob stopped dragging him, they finished him off within minutes.

I thought of a Muslim woman who was a teacher at my college. When her five children were still small, her husband died. A year after being widowed, she announced that she wanted to marry a Christian man. People gathered in the street to protest, screaming that she was wrong to marry an infidel. She stood on the street with her children, begging the crowd not to hurt her or her family. She promised to abandon her plans of marriage, but after that she was never accepted back into the community. She lost her job, her home—everything.

When I was a child, there was a woman I knew who had converted from Christianity to Islam when she got married. She was considered a pariah, an outsider. Nobody would accept the food she sent around as gifts from house to house. Even though the cooked almonds and cashews in milk smelled delicious, my mother told me not to touch it. "The blood inside is Christian blood," she said. And when this woman's children were of marrying age, no one would marry them. There was no mercy for her. Ever.

✝

I stood at the front of the church and looked at the pastor. He seemed nervous.

"You're sure nobody saw you come here?"

"I'm sure," John said.

The pastor looked at me. "And you told nobody?"

"Nobody," I said.

He bit his lip and checked the window for the third time since we had walked in.

"Please," I said, "when I die, I want to die as a Christian. I want to be baptized. Nobody but us will ever know."

He looked at John and then back at me. "Okay," he said. "But we'll do this quickly."

He spoke a little about what baptism means, about the prayers he would lead me in, and how he would use water to mark my head with the sign of the cross. When he was finished explaining everything, he paused. "It's common for people with Muslim names to choose a new name when they become Christians. What name do you want to be known by?"

"That's easy," I said. "From now on I want to be called Esther."

✝

The next day, a Thursday, I woke up late, but I woke up ready. I hadn't thought I was scared before, but as I sat on my bed and let my mind delight in what it would be like to stand face-to-face with Jesus, I realized I had lost the final traces of fear that had been clinging to me.

My baptism had been a simple ceremony. I had cried through much of it, though not out of fear or sadness. Warm, heavy tears had fallen from my cheeks for one simple reason: love. If ever I had wondered whether Jesus could love a sinner like me, my baptism banished doubt forever. I don't know how, but I knew: God's love for me was real.

I had gone to sleep with the peace of God resting heavily on me, and I had woken up feeling just the same.

"I'm a child of your Kingdom now," I said aloud to my empty bedroom. "There's nothing about death that scares me."

No debate was scheduled for that day, and I walked downstairs, expecting it to be quiet. It was not. Curious, I went to see who was in the meeting room.

My father was talking with Anwar and a dozen or more other clerics. They did not see me at first, and I knew exactly what they were talking about. Words like *jihad* and *heaven* and *kafir* carried across the room.

"You should talk to him," I said, pointing at Anwar. The conversation stopped, and everyone turned to look at me. "He's the one who first told me that the Bible can teach us about the prophets. Isn't that right?"

"Yes," he said. "I did."

Before I could say anything else, my father marched toward me and shut the door.

An hour later, my mother came to my room, sobbing. "I heard them as they were leaving. They said that you aren't coming back to Islam. They'll kill you tomorrow after prayers."

Her sobbing grew louder. I tried to comfort her, telling her that it was okay, that we had both known this would happen.

From the moment I'd become a Christian, I had known that I'd be punished and that nobody would ever accept me again. There is no grace, no mercy, no love in Islam.

When my mother caught her breath, she spoke softly. "They said they'll give you such an exemplary death that nobody in Pakistan will ever try to follow your footsteps. They're telling your father that children are given by God and that killing you is doing the will of Allah. This is his jihad—if he kills you himself, he will go straight to heaven when he dies."

Yes, I thought. *Of course they'd say that.* The promise of avoiding judgment and gaining Allah's favor was such a potent motivator. It had been strong enough for me to consider being a suicide bomber and strong enough to turn the man who gave me life into my murderer.

"It's okay, Ami. You're a Christian, and so are three of your children. If I stay firm until the point of death, I believe that many more people will come to know Jesus too. If my death brings more people to him, I'm happy. Jesus' death brought many to him, and Paul and nearly all the other apostles endured painful deaths. It was all part of God's plan. Maybe this is his plan for me."

She looked at me, and fresh tears streaked her face.

"I just want to stay firm until the end."

†

I spent hours reading a book John had given me. He said that the usual gift for new converts was a copy of the Holy Bible, but he had chosen something different for me. It was a book about Christian martyrs.

The sunlight tracked across my room as I fed on those stories. Some Christians had been skinned alive, some had been stoned, and some had endured deaths so brutal I couldn't even conceive of how someone would come up with such an idea. But surprisingly, with every story I read, I found myself more at peace. I would soon be with the Lord.

Would he take my spirit to be with him while my father did things to my body? Or would I remain in my flesh until the very end? Whatever I experienced, I knew it would not compare to what Jesus went through. Even if I was lashed and spit on, taunted and beaten, I vowed to take my suffering quietly, just like my Savior did.

"Lord," I prayed, "however many drops of my blood are spilled, let that be the number of souls that come to you through my death."

†

My mother touched my arm, breaking my focus on what I was reading.

"This isn't right," she whispered. "I can't stand to see people kill you. I gave birth to you. It isn't right."

"Ami, it's okay. I'm under blasphemy for leaving Islam and declaring my love for Jesus. They will kill me. It would be madness to think they might change their minds."

"Well, I don't agree. I want to help you escape."

"No," I said. "What if someone sees me? They will give me a private death, and what would the point of that be? And I don't want people to think I'm running away in fear."

"Nobody thinks you're afraid, Zakhira. You've stood up and debated them all. But if you run and escape, then maybe God will save you so you can tell many more people about Jesus."

"You really think so?"

She nodded.

I felt my breath grow heavy within me, just like the time I

woke up from the dream when I met Jesus. The sense of peace was stronger than ever.

"Okay," I said. "If it really is God's will, I guess I'll make it out."

Part 4

GO TO ANOTHER LAND THAT GOD WILL GIVE YOU

24

I woke to the feeling of someone touching my shoulder. My mother leaned over and whispered so quietly that I could just barely hear. "It's nearly 2 a.m.," she said. "You have to go."

I followed her out of my room and to the back door. *Lord, I prayed with every step, keep my father in a deep sleep.* My mother eased the lock open, handed me my schoolbag, which I always kept by the door, and pulled me to her to say good-bye. When she spoke, her breath was warm against my ear. "I might never see you again," she said. She fought hard to swallow her tears. We both did. Neither of us wanted to make any more noise than we had to.

She closed the door quickly behind me. We lived in a busy part of town, and I had never experienced such a deep silence in the streets. I slipped through the metal gates and looked both ways, scanning the pools of light cast by the streetlights. Nothing moved. The world was on pause.

I took a few steps but stopped when I saw a car cross the intersection at the end of the road. Had I been spotted? I listened, but the sound of the car's engine faded away.

Pulling my head scarf tighter, I started walking again. I crossed the road to avoid streetlights and paused on the few occasions when I heard a car. I was tempted to give in to the panic that surged within me and break into a run, but I knew I couldn't. I calmed myself by trying to remember the items I had in my bag. Some pocket money. My high school diploma. A few pens. My copy of the Qur'an, covered with highlighter ink and scribbled notes. For some reason it had not occurred to me to pack any clothes.

I hadn't had time to think through any of this. Once my mother had persuaded me to escape, the final hours of the day had been a blur. She'd managed to get my father out of the house for a few minutes, giving me enough time to call John at work.

"I'm in trouble," I told him. "My mother will get me out of my house, but I need to go soon. Can you help me?"

"Okay." His words were clear and firm—there was no hesitation in his voice. "What can I do?"

"Meet me tonight at 2:15 near the tree outside the old infant school. If you see I'm being followed, ignore me and drive off."

With every step I took, I thanked God for John. I had a death sentence hanging over my head, but nobody knew anything about John. He was risking everything for me.

I thanked God for my mother, too. I tried not to imagine what would happen when my father woke up. If he suspected that she was involved in my escape in any way, he would turn the full force of his rage on her.

As I turned a corner, I saw that John was waiting. I was

desperate to look behind me to see if I was being followed. John stayed where he was, looking left and right, straining his neck to look behind me. When I was about a hundred feet from him, I started running.

"Let's go," he said. He pointed me toward his motorbike, which was parked on a side street.

We rode across the city, and after a few minutes, I stopped watching where we were going. I closed my eyes and held on to the back of the bike, resting my head against John's back. I could feel him turning around constantly to make sure we weren't being followed.

When we finally stopped and John cut the engine, we were in a part of the city I had never seen before. I followed him through a narrow alley and up some stairs to a small apartment. John introduced me to a man and a woman in their twenties who told me I could stay with them for a few days. They assured me that I didn't have to tell them anything about what had happened to me. I suddenly felt shy and vulnerable, even though their kindness was unmistakable.

"You can sleep in here," the husband said quietly, showing me a room where his three young daughters lay asleep on floor mats.

"We're Christians too," he said. "You're safe here."

I sat on a spare mat and listened to the low murmurs as John talked with the man in the next room. I looked over at the girls, who slept with their arms and legs draped over each other. They were barely old enough to attend school.

I felt even younger than the smallest one of them, weak and vulnerable. I'd been ripped from the protection of my mother. I had never felt so alone.

I tried to clear my head to pray. I thanked God for this kind, brave family. I thanked him for saving me and asked him to continue to protect me. As I drifted off to sleep, I tried to keep my fears at bay. *Did Paul and the apostles ever feel this way?* I wondered.

†

"Please, find a husband. Get married." Those were some of the last words my mother had said to me as we embraced by the door the night before. As the girls' bedroom filled with sunlight and my fears began to subside, my mother's plea came back to me.

As I thought about the future that lay before me, I knew my mother was right. It would be hard enough for me to survive in Pakistan as a single woman, and it would be almost impossible for me to make it on the run. But how could I get married? Who would have me?

There was only one person I could ask.

When John arrived later that morning with fresh naan and sweet chai for me, I waited for the right moment. He asked me how I'd slept, and I told him how kind my hosts were. Then we ate and drank in silence. My insides were twisted so tight that I was not hungry at all, but I forced down tiny mouthfuls.

I was safe, but I'd never before felt so vulnerable. I was surrounded by people I could be completely open with about my faith, yet I had never felt so alone.

"Please," I said when the silence grew heavy between us, "I have no choice. My mother told me not to live with a man, and she wants me to get married. If you could marry me, it would help me so much."

I watched a smile begin to play across John's face. Then he got a serious look and took a deep breath. I prepared myself for rejection, my eyes dropping to the morsel of bread in my hands. In Pakistan, women simply did not propose to men.

What was I thinking, asking him such a question? And why would a Christian like John accept a woman like me?

"Yes," he said. "I will marry you."

I looked up. The same serious expression was there, but his voice was full of warmth and love.

"I've liked you ever since you started asking me for a Bible," he said. "But you never said anything."

For a moment I didn't know what to say. I liked him too, but I had buried my feelings deep inside. Never had I dared to hope that he would accept me.

We started to talk about the details. John said he would need to meet with his mother and his pastor, since his father was dead. We did not need the permission of John's family and church, but we wanted their blessing—and their protection.

I was still in a daze. Was I really getting married—and to a Christian man?

After John left to talk with his pastor, I spent the day in the apartment on my own. I borrowed a Bible and lost myself in its pages.

When John returned later in the day, he looked anxious. "My pastor won't marry us," he said. "He says it's too dangerous for the rest of the congregation."

We sat in silence for a while.

"What about your mother?" I asked.

"I talked to her and some of my friends, and they're all concerned for me. But I'm not worried about them—just my pastor. If he doesn't agree to marry us, we'll have to get a court marriage. Are you prepared for that?"

I was. A public ceremony would mean more risk, but we had little choice. Even so, I did not want to give up on the idea of a Christian wedding so easily. For years I had wanted to get married in a white dress, and now that I had left behind so much of my old life, this one dream felt like something worth fighting for. There would be no crowds or extended celebrations like in a traditional Muslim wedding, but that did not matter. I wanted to start my marriage by standing before God, making our vows in his house. That was what mattered most.

"What if I spoke with your pastor?"

John agreed, and after a phone call to the pastor, the two of us took the short ride over to the church.

"Pastor," I said as I stood in front of him, trying to persuade him once again to put himself and his congregation at risk. "It says in the Holy Bible that God is like the shepherd who has one hundred sheep. When one is lost, he leaves the ninety-nine and goes in search of the one.[24] I am the one. He came and found me—he rescued me. But I'm not safely home yet. So please, would you marry us?"

The pastor wiped the tears from his eyes and looked at John and then back at me. "You have to promise that you won't tell anyone I've done this."

"I promise," I said.

"You're not going to tell your family where you got married?"

"I promise," I said. "I won't tell anyone."

†

After the flurry of the past couple of days—fleeing from home on Thursday night and proposing to John on Friday—I faced a whole week of waiting until we could get married. I wanted to have the ceremony sooner, but the pastor insisted that we hold the ceremony when the streets were at their emptiest. So we waited until the end of the week, when the mosques were full of faithful Muslims attending Friday prayers.

I continued to stay in the apartment with John's friends, and the wife brought a selection of wedding dresses for me to try on. In those moments, with white, flowing dresses filling the cramped bedroom and the young girls giggling shyly until their mother shooed them away, I almost felt like a carefree teenager again.

But my secret was never far from the surface. For the family's safety, I told them nothing of my former life, other than that I had run away from home. Even John did not know the full story of how close I had come to strapping on a suicide vest and murdering innocent Christians like him and the kind family who now offered me shelter.

Should I tell him? I wrestled with the question all week long. There was a part of me that wanted to tell him everything about my past—to begin our marriage without secrets. But how could I expect him to understand the darkness I had come from and the way my heart had been twisted by pain, lies, and hatred when John and I knew so little about each other as it was?

In the end, I decided to wait. I promised myself that I would tell him everything as soon as the time was right.

†

The closer we got to our wedding day, the more I reminisced about the weddings of my two older sisters. Both had been lavish events, with hundreds of people celebrating over several days. Memories of the food and the music, the colors and the crowds filled my senses. I'd never seen my father as happy as he was at both of those events.

My wedding could not have been more different. Only a handful of people were there: John's mother and brother and the friends whose apartment I had been staying in. We had to make the ceremony quick and quiet, and there were moments when I looked down at my white dress and felt a little self-conscious. Why had I chosen the whitest, most billowing skirt when I was about to be married in front of strangers?

I missed my mom, too. It felt wrong that she and my siblings were not present, doubly wrong that none of them even knew the ceremony was taking place. But for everyone's safety, my family's absence was a price worth paying.

In the end, my nerves and faint whispers of melancholy dispersed. I looked at John as he turned to me and told me that he would take me as his wife from this day forward.

When it was my turn to speak, my voice was quiet. Not out of doubt or fear, but because of the solemn weight of the words. "For better, for worse, for richer, for poorer, in sickness and in health, to love and to cherish, till death us do part."

It seemed strange to talk about death on the day we married, especially knowing the threats that were close behind me. But to do so together, knowing that we would face whatever lay ahead side by side, changed something deep within me. I was no longer alone. God had brought the perfect man along to be my partner. Finally, at long last, I was safe.

†

After the wedding, we moved in with John's mother. I was grateful to have someone to call *ami* after leaving my home in such an abrupt way. But I was also glad to have her fill in some of the many blank spaces in my knowledge about the man I had just married.

I listened in awe as she described what he had been like as a child. "John wasn't like the other children in our village," she said. "Even among the Christians in our community, he stood out."

While other believers kept quiet about their faith, John saw no reason to hide. Instead, he boldly proclaimed his love for Jesus. She shared story after story while John sat to one side, smiling politely and waving the air with his hand whenever he grew embarrassed by the attention. I cherished every moment.

Of all the stories about John's past, one stood out as my clear favorite. John was only five years old at the time, but his courage and passion eclipsed that of most adults I knew. When he began to understand that Muslims and Christians had profoundly different views on Jesus, he decided to do something about it.

One Friday afternoon, he slipped out of his home and made the short walk to the local mosque. He was holding a Bible in his hands.

When the leaders at the mosque saw him holding the Holy Bible, they asked, "What is this?"

"It's my Bible, and I want to read it inside," John said.

One of the leaders saw John's mother coming toward him and said, "Go back to your home."

At this point John's mother got a thoughtful look on her face. "I believe this was a sign for his father and me," she said. "God had a plan for John's future."

In the years that followed, John continued in much the same way, living with courage and a sense of freedom that many other Christians in Pakistan lacked. John's parents continued to encourage him, teaching him and his brother how to apply the Bible to real life.

When John was old enough to read for himself, he began to see what Jesus, the disciples, and the apostle Paul had in common: they were beaten, jailed, and killed in their service to God. It was a revelation that had a lasting impact on him, filling him with courage and compassion, and teaching him to listen for God's voice, even if it meant risking his life.

✝

My hand shook as I dialed the number.

In the week since our wedding, I had begun to tell John a little about my father. I explained how angry he was that I had turned my back on Islam, and I told him a little about the debates. I shared with him my hope that now that I was a wife and the responsibility of another man, perhaps my father would feel less obligated to make a public example of me. "If he no longer feels responsible for me, then maybe he'll accept who I am now."

John listened, nodding gently.

"Perhaps he'll allow me to return home for a visit," I added. "Maybe the Lord will soften his heart, just as he did with my mother, sister, and brother."

We decided I would call home and share my news. It seemed so simple when we talked about it, but as I waited for someone to pick up, I felt anxiety clamp my throat.

"Hello?"

I sighed with relief. We had not been apart that long, but I drew such comfort from hearing my mother's voice. "Hello, Ami," I said. "I have some news for you. I got married! To John, the man who told me about Jesus."

"That's really good, Zakhira. I'm so happy! Are you happy?"

"Yes!" I laughed. "I'm happy." I paused, knowing what I needed to say next. "Can I talk to Father?"

He came to the phone more quickly than I anticipated. When he said hello, his tone was impossible to read.

"I got married," I said. "To a Christian man."

"A Christian man?" His voice was warm and friendly, which surprised me. "That's good. That's really good. What is our son-in-law's name?"

"John."

"John. That's a good name. And does he have a job? We need to make sure that he can look after you!"

"Yes, he has a good job in a medical lab."

"That's good. And where are you living? Is this your new phone number?"

I told him which part of the city we were in and that he could call anytime. It felt so good to be able to talk to him like this. It had been years since we'd spoken for so long. And not since the days of panda ice cream had I sensed such warmth in his attitude toward me.

I decided to take a risk.

"Can I come and see you? If you'll allow it, I would like to come and see you and Ami and everyone else."

"Yes! Of course you can come. And bring our son-in-law with you. We must meet him. Come tomorrow night."

When I came back into the bedroom, John looked at me, trying to read my face. "Well?" he said. "Did you talk to your father?"

"Yes," I said, feeling confused by the conversation.

"Is your family okay?"

"Yes, I think they are. He said we can visit them. Tomorrow."

"That's good, right?"

†

The next day John was in the shower and I was fixing my hair, getting ready to head to my parents' home, when the phone rang.

It was my mother.

"Don't come here." Her words came out in a rush. "Your father took down all the details you told him, and he has people gathering downstairs. They have pistols. They're talking about killing you both. You cannot stay wherever you are. You have to run!"

She ended the call before I could say anything in response, but even if she had stayed on the line, I doubt I could have found any words to say. I felt hollowed out. The hope that I'd clung to since leaving home in the middle of the night had been ripped from my heart. And now it was not just my life that was in danger; it was John's as well.

I knocked on the bathroom door. "John?" I said. "We can't go."

I told him about the call, trying to rein in the panic. John looked worried, but as soon as I was done talking, he pulled out two bags from behind the door. He filled them with a few of his clothes, along with all the items he'd bought for me in the previous week.

"We have to go now."

Thirty minutes later, I once again found myself standing in front of an open door, hugging a woman and saying good-bye. This time it was John's mother who was crying with me.

"If they come here," John said, "tell them that we left many days ago and that you don't know where we are."

Minutes later, we were in a rickshaw, heading for the train station. Within the hour, our train was pulling out of the city, putting the first of nine hundred miles between us and my father. A sunset flooded the carriage with the colors of fire. John and I watched in silence as we made our way through flat, wide lands dotted with single-story houses and small farms. I squeezed his hand. "It will all be okay now, won't it?"

"Of course," he said. "I'll take care of you."

25

John's aunt offered us a room in her home on the outskirts of Quetta. To her we were just a couple of happy newlyweds enjoying an extended honeymoon. Even though my home was eighteen hours away, John and I agreed that it was better for his aunt to know as little as possible about my background. Since I dressed like a Christian and went by my Christian name, we let John's aunt and family assume that my background was just like theirs. John and I agreed that it was safer that way.

Several weeks into our stay, I discovered I was pregnant. We were delighted. John soon found work in a nearby medical lab, while I spent my days studying the Bible, resting, and thinking about the future that lay ahead for the three of us.

As the heat of summer grew more intense, I made a habit of reading Scripture to the baby growing within me. I would work through Revelation and preach about the future that awaited us, or I'd read Psalm 103 and give thanks for all the blessings God had given us. Sometimes, when John and I were the only ones in the house, I would walk the cool-tiled floor and sing the worship songs I had learned as a secret believer. John would cover his ears in mock pain over my off-key singing, and we'd laugh. Then I would go right back to singing.

John got a reasonable salary with his new job, and he had plenty of savings, yet we knew we had to be careful with our money, especially since we wanted to move into a place of our own before the baby arrived. His aunt advised us to spread out our costs by buying baby clothes and supplies in the months leading up to the birth.

As soon as we had our ultrasound in the second trimester and found out we were having a girl, I started shopping. There was a market just a short bus ride away, and we made a habit of visiting there every time John got paid. I would look for clothes while John wandered among the stalls that sold everything from diapers to strollers.

One day, when my belly had grown large enough for the stallholders to notice I was pregnant and inflate their prices accordingly, I heard someone call my name. Not Esther, the Christian name I used with every person I'd met since I was baptized, but Zakhira, the name my father had given me.

I turned, and just ten feet away from me was one of my father's sisters. I had not seen her for years—not since a family wedding back when I had been a dutiful Muslim daughter. But there was no mistaking her. And as she pointed an accusatory finger at me, it was clear that she recognized me too.

"It *is* you!" She walked up to me, her gaze fierce. For a moment I feared she was going to strike me, but when she got a few feet from me, she suddenly pulled back, as if afraid to get too close. "They are looking for you at home. I will tell your father you are here."

I thought about trying to convince her that the whole thing was a misunderstanding. I thought about begging her not to say anything. If I started pleading, would it make any difference? If I lied, would she believe me? It would never work, and I knew it.

So I ran.

The market was not as big as those back home, but it was crowded. I had to push my way through the crowds, one hand clearing the way ahead, the other protecting my unborn child.

After taking several wrong turns, I finally found John.

"What is it?" he asked.

"Please come." I was so out of breath I could barely get the words out. "We need to leave Quetta right now."

"Why?"

"Let's go first. I'll tell you on the way."

"Has someone found you?"

"Yes."

We took the first bus back and cleared out of his aunt's house. By evening, we were on another train.

†

I assumed that life would carry on much as it had. I hoped that we would find a new place to live and that John would get a new job. Then we would settle down in preparation for our baby's birth. I knew we would probably never return home, but I hoped we would at least be able to make a new life for ourselves, much like we were beginning to do in Quetta.

I was wrong. John called his various cousins, aunts, and uncles, but none of them would let us stay with them for any length of time. They had all heard I was a former Muslim, and none of them wanted to place their own families at risk. We spent almost two weeks shuttling from place to place, but we knew this could not last.

We had savings, but nowhere near enough to rent a place to live on our own. We could pay for our own food, but we needed to rely on the generosity of others to put a roof over our heads. Besides, without the protection of family, we knew we could not live as a Christian couple in a Muslim area. And with names like John and Esther, people would know right away that we were not Muslims. We needed to live quietly, away from prying eyes. We needed to disappear.

†

I had spent hardly any time in a Christian neighborhood before. When I was a secret believer living at home, I would offer food and water to the Christians who swept the street. I knew they were poor and guessed that their homes were in parts of the city that people from my neighborhood would never go near. I knew a little about the conditions some of these people lived in, but I had never seen the depths of their poverty with my own eyes.

As soon as we ran out of family to stay with, I experienced it for myself.

Ali, one of John's friends, offered to let us stay with him until the baby was born, and one afternoon when I was seven months pregnant, we made the long walk from the train station to his home. I was tired from the heat of the sun, my body protesting with all manner of aches and pains. As soon as I saw Ali's home, I felt a whole lot worse.

There was an open sewer running outside, and the inside was not much better. The single room was dark and damp, and there was no electricity and no running water. An old, faded curtain hung limply from the ceiling. From what I gathered, this curtain would partition off the corner of the room that would be ours. The area was no bigger than the two sleeping mats that were stacked against the wall.

Nothing in my life so far had prepared me for this. I'd grown up the daughter of a successful merchant in a wealthy northern city. John's family was not as well off as my family, but they had cars and cell phones, access to higher education, and jobs that offered stability. Neither of us had ever known hunger. Ali's home, which he shared with his wife and four children—and now us as well—seemed to belong on a different planet.

As Christians, Ali and his neighbors were the victims of continual discrimination. They struggled to find jobs, their businesses were boycotted by Muslims, and their children were unable to access education. Even those like Ali, who had been educated before converting from Islam, were barred from employment. They were viewed as toxic in their community, living like lepers. Some families relied on the meager wage of one person working a menial job, and others had friends and family overseas who were willing to help.

Even so, they saw themselves as fortunate. Ali described a neighboring community of Christians whose homes had been bulldozed with barely any warning so a developer could build on the land. They were given no money, no support, and no help to find another place to live. All they could do was find an unused corner of a slum and try to construct new homes out of trash.

Ali also told me about one Christian man he knew of who, against the odds, had managed to get a job working in a factory. Almost all of his fellow workers were Muslims. The man was good at his job, and one day, after years of working hard, he was told he would be promoted to section manager. That night, two men with pistols shot him inside his own home. "How can a Christian manage us?" they shouted before they walked away.

The pain these Christians were living with was palpable. But their generosity was even greater. Ali and his family shared their home with John and me, and the community welcomed us warmly. Though the thought of giving birth in the middle of such poverty scared me at first, I trusted that God was in control.

†

A few weeks before giving birth to our daughter, we moved away from Ali's home. A friend who worked at a Christian college in our home city invited us to stay in the basement while the college was closed for the students' vacation. I was unsure about being so close to danger, but the idea of giving birth in a clean environment, close to a hospital, was appealing.

We moved in at night, being careful not to attract any attention. John was brave enough to leave the basement to run errands and visit other Christians, but I stayed inside with the door locked. There was a bed and clean water—I had all I needed.

While I was grateful to be somewhere clean, I felt incredibly alone. I missed having Christians around me, and I missed my family. I longed for my mom and my aunts, my sisters and my cousins to be with me, to fill the air with laughter and conversation. I wanted to give birth the way every other woman in my family had: surrounded by relatives.

By the time my labor started, I was beginning to feel fearful. Soon I was in agony.

John had found a Christian nurse who agreed to help me,

and while I labored in pain with no sign that the birth was progressing, the nurse gave me this warning: "If something doesn't change soon, we'll need to go to the hospital."

I was desperate not to go, worried that if I left the basement, I would be seen by someone who knew me. So I prayed. "God, you promised you would help. Have you left me?"

Almost that very minute, I felt something change in my body. The pain vanished, and within an hour, I was holding her—a beautiful daughter we named Amiyah. As I stared at her mop of dark hair and deep eyes, I thanked God for his assurance and his help. I knew that I had been wrong to ever doubt him.

John's response to a daughter could not have been more different from my father's. The moment he first held his baby girl, his face was wet with tears. "My father always wanted a daughter," he said. "He loved his sons, but he always said that to have a daughter is a special blessing."

The nurse left soon after, and the three of us lay on the bed for hours, soaking in God's faithfulness in the form of this eight-pound bundle. It was dark in the basement, but I knew we were safe.

26

Two weeks after Amiyah's birth, we had to leave the college. We were grateful that a friend of John's arranged for us to stay with a Christian family about an hour away, but the conditions were even worse than at Ali's.

As we tried to settle into our new life, I discovered that becoming a mother brought new worries and fears. I missed my mother more than ever. I wished I could ask for her advice about feeding and bathing, and it made me ache knowing that she would miss Amiyah's first steps and never hear her first words. I also grew concerned that Amiyah might get ill. How would we take care of her if we were on the run and had no income? Other worries plagued me too, like the thought of what might happen to our daughter if my father tracked me down and killed both John and me.

With John's family also at risk, we decided that if anything happened to us, the best people to look after Amiyah were the

Christians we were living with. They might have been poor and
on the margins of society, but I came to see how much I could
learn from them. In the midst of all the hardship they faced,
I discovered the truth about so many Christians in Pakistan:
their faith in Jesus is strong. They have so little to eat and so
little to cling to that they are forced to rely on God alone.

They taught me about being faithful, about not denying
the faith. At any point, they could have converted to Islam
and found their status elevated, yet they chose to remain poor
followers of Jesus, even though they and their children faced a
lifetime of social, emotional, and physical persecution. My suffering was small by comparison, and I believed that in time it
would pass. Theirs was permanent. I was reminded once more
that Christians suffer. Because of Jesus' name, we become the
recipients of hatred. This should not surprise us—after all,
Jesus came from a higher place, yet he chose to humble himself. He chose to suffer here on earth.

✝

We continued to move around, traveling only at night, with
my face hidden beneath a veil and John's covered by a ban-
danna. At times I thought about the apostles Paul and Peter,
and how they went from place to place, often being smuggled
in and out of cities. What was so different about what we were
going through? In many ways, it was comforting to know that
we were living out the truths of the Bible.

As Amiyah grew, my understanding of God became ever
stronger. Knowing the depth of my own love for my child
and watching John care for his daughter gave me new insight
into what the love of the heavenly Father looks like. And as
difficult as it was to watch God's people suffer, I was thankful
for the privilege of learning from them how to keep the faith

when hard times come. I didn't know what lay ahead for our family, but I had a hunch this was a lesson I was going to need.

For a few precious weeks, we started to feel settled, and I wondered whether we might consider ourselves finally home. Then we received some shocking news. An old friend contacted John to tell him that his mother was dead.

My father had printed up posters with our pictures on them, along with the instruction that anyone who found us should kill us. Somehow John's mother had seen a copy of the poster, and the shock had been too much. She had a heart attack and died soon after.

John's grief was intensified all the more by the fact that he could not attend the funeral. I felt the weight of guilt press down on me. Marrying me had already cost him his career, his home, and the opportunity to live near his family. Now it had robbed his mother of her own life.

But John never showed any sign of resentment or regret over marrying me. With every new challenge that came, he stood by my side and made sure we faced it together.

†

Amiyah was napping when the man who had taken us into his home burst through the door, panting.

"I just saw a man . . . holding a poster . . . with your faces on it."

"Where?" John asked.

"The train station. He's asking everyone whether they've seen you."

It was as if someone had clamped a vice around my throat, cutting off the air. We were hundreds of miles away from home, and two years had passed since I'd escaped. I desperately wanted to believe this was all some strange coincidence. I had hoped my father's anger had mellowed over time, but clearly that was a fantasy.

"Stay here," the man said. "Lock the door, and don't go anywhere. We'll keep watch outside. We won't let them hurt you. But once they're gone, you should leave."

We got out of the city that night, but it took another three months for us to leave Pakistan altogether. We shuttled from one Christian community to another, all the while trying to plan an escape.

The main problem, as usual, was me. I had no passport or travel papers with me, and without them I could not leave Pakistan or enter any other country legally. In a way, though, I was grateful my father had never allowed me to have any kind of photo ID. He said he did not want his daughter to have her photograph taken and printed, and it would be up to my husband one day to decide whether I got an ID once I got married. If my father had been less militant, I might never have been able to leave Pakistan, for any formal ID would have made it clear I was a Muslim. If I had tried to get a passport with such an ID, Pakistani officials would want to know why a Muslim woman was planning to leave the country with a Christian man, especially when there was a child involved.

So I had to forget about my previous life when I went to apply for a passport. I pretended that I was a shy, illiterate girl from a remote village. I gave my thumbprint, and after waiting for several weeks, I finally received my passport.

†

Malaysia was not my first choice. I wanted to fly to a country with a large Christian population, not another Muslim country, but our choices were limited. All other doors were closed to us, so Malaysia became our new home.

On our first Sunday in the country, John, Amiyah, and I left the center for asylum seekers, where we had been given temporary accommodations, and took an hour-long journey across Kuala Lumpur. I stared openmouthed at the glass and steel high-rises and smiled at the cleanliness of the bus. But these were only brief distractions. My heart was focused on one thing: the unrelenting joy of going to church.

After more than two years of living on the run in Pakistan, the thought of being able to worship alongside a thousand other Christians was almost too much to take in. I'd attended a few church services in Pakistan, but I'd never been in a congregation close to this size. I could feel my heart racing as we approached the building, and when I saw that the pastor was greeting people at the door, I didn't know whether to clasp my hands together and bow or giggle out of nervousness.

"Welcome!" he said, smiling broadly. "What a beautiful child you have."

"Thank you," John said. "This is our first time here. We're from Pakistan."

"Really? Then you are especially welcome. Why did you leave?"

John looked quickly at me, then back at the pastor. "My wife was a Muslim but now loves the Lord. It was safer for us to come to Malaysia."

The pastor turned his gaze on me, his smile still wide. "Ex-terrorist!" he said, jabbing a finger toward me.

My heart stopped. I suddenly felt faint. I heard John laugh a little and wish the pastor good day, and then I felt his hand on my arm, guiding me into the building.

"People shouldn't stereotype Muslims like that," John said softly when we sat down. "It's not right, and I'm sorry you had to hear that."

Amiyah needed to visit the bathroom, and John took her. I sat in the pew alone, waves of panic tearing at my insides.

Why had the pastor said that? Had God revealed my secret to him? If he had, was he about to reveal it to the rest of the church as well? What would I do if the pastor asked me to stand up and walk forward in front of everyone? If John found out, I was sure it would mean the end of our marriage.

I sat through the whole service begging God not to let that happen. I confessed to God that I was nothing more than trash, that I had been so lost in the darkness that I was not worthy to stand and touch his feet. I was lower than everyone else in the building, but I begged to be allowed to remain there.

The pastor said nothing about me during the service, and when he said good-bye afterward, it was as if he'd never seen either of us before.

All the way back to the refugee camp, while John and Amiyah dozed in the sunlight that flooded through the bus windows, I tried to ignore the blood rushing in my ears as I thanked God for the narrow escape. However, in the silence, I sensed that God wasn't cheering along with me. What had happened that morning was not a rescue; it was a warning. Though I wished it weren't so, he was reminding me of a truth I had forgotten: nothing we do can ever be hidden from him.

It was a difficult revelation. I knew I could trust him to keep my family safe just as he had done so many times before. But letting go of the need for secrets was hard. I begged God not to reveal my past to others.

"Please," I prayed. "I promise I'll spend my whole life serving you, but I'm terrified of what might happen if people find out about me. Do they really have to know?"

27

When I was a child, my father would sometimes let me count the money he brought home after selling spices. I would sit at the table, my eyes level with the piles of bills that covered the surface like autumn leaves. At first I was only allowed to handle the low-value bills, counting them out until I had the right amount to pass over to my father. He'd roll up the pile and fasten it with a rubber band, and I'd watch him load the cash into the safe.

The more I did this, the higher the value of the bills I was allowed to handle. At the time, it didn't occur to me that I was counting thousands of dollars' worth of currency. I just liked being able to help my father.

Years later, when I was a secret believer, my father was out of the country on business. He and my mother each had a key to the safe, but he had accidentally taken both keys with him. I needed money to take a rickshaw to college and buy lunch before visiting John, but there was no way to open the safe to get the cash.

I had been a Christian for only a few weeks, but I knew what I needed to do. "God," I prayed that night, "when there was no sun, you spoke and it came into being. The world started at your command. You gathered the waters and raised the land. I have no money to get to college and visit John tomorrow, and I desperately want to study the Holy Bible more. Please, can you help?"

The next morning I woke with my hand clenched. I knew without a doubt what would be in my palm even before I peeled back my fingers. Sure enough, it was the exact amount of money I needed.

I rushed to my mother. "Did you give me money last night?" I asked.

She assured me she hadn't. The whole incident confused her, but I knew exactly what had happened: God had provided.

I thought about that event a lot when we were getting settled in Malaysia. Even though we were no longer living in fear and poverty, we were still desperately short on money. We had used most of our savings to pay for airfare out of Pakistan, and being asylum seekers, we were not officially allowed to work, so the little cash we had left was soon gone.

In some ways, life in Malaysia was even harder than being on the run in Pakistan. Now we couldn't run to different Christian communities for help. We were no longer unique— we were just a few out of thousands of asylum seekers, part of an anonymous invasion that many people in the country did not welcome.

Malaysia is a Muslim country, but there were some advantages to being there. Not only did this destination raise fewer suspicions for the Pakistani border guards, but we also believed we'd stand a better chance of our case being heard there than in a place like Hong Kong, which I had preferred. We knew that a complex process lay ahead of us, but we hoped we'd be granted refugee status fairly soon. After that, our goal was to apply through the United Nations to be relocated to a Christian country.

As the weeks rolled into months and our application seemed to have stalled right at the early stages, it became clear that the process was even slower and more complex than we had assumed.

We didn't need just one miracle. We needed a series of them.

†

John was often quiet during those early months, and that worried me. Sometimes several days went by when he would hardly speak to me or Amiyah. I sensed that he was becoming distant and preoccupied.

When Amiyah was asleep early one morning, I brought him some sweet chai and held his hand. "I feel bad for all the sacrifices you've made," I said. "You deserve more security than this, and less fear."

He smiled at me, but the silence remained.

I took a deep breath. The words I needed to say were bunched up in my throat, resisting my efforts. When I finally spoke, my voice was as timid as a fearful child's. "If you want to leave, I'll understand."

"No," he said immediately. "No, Esther. I'm happy—truly, I am."

"Really? Sometimes you seem sad, and it makes me sad too."

He paused for a moment, searching for the right words. "It's not easy living this way, and it's not the life I wanted to give you and Amiyah. But I know that this is all for the Lord. This is what he wants for us right now. If this is his will, then I want to follow him. Is that what you want too?"

"Yes!" I said. "I want to live all for God, with you beside me."

"Me too," he said, taking my hand in his and smiling for the first time in days. "All for God. You and me."

God, I prayed, *what have I done to deserve such a wonderful Christian husband?*

†

It did not happen overnight, the way God had provided my rickshaw fare, but God did meet our needs. John was offered work looking after an elderly, bedridden patient, and we were able to move out of the refugee center and into the free accommodation provided by his job.

We were grateful to have a place to stay, but John's pay was modest, and money remained tight. There were many times when I'd look at the empty kitchen cupboards, wondering what I would feed our family that evening.

I'd bow down on the floor and call out to God, "Lord, you know everything, and you know I have nothing to feed my husband or my little girl, but still I will show you." I would get up and throw open all the cupboards. "See? There's nothing here. I'm asking for my daily bread. Would you please provide for us? I know you promised to carry us in your hand, and I know you alone are the one true God. Please prove yourself faithful to us."

God never failed to reply. Sometimes he did so quietly, without much fanfare, and John would return home from work with enough money for us to eat for a few days. Other times God's intervention was almost breathtaking.

One day, when I was staring at the open cupboards and

reminding God that we really needed help, there was a knock at the door. I opened it to see two women, one of them an Indonesian woman from the apartment below ours. She did not know any English, and the two of us had communicated only by sign language in the past. She waved hello and then had me talk to the other woman, who was holding two large shopping bags.

"Hello," the stranger said. "I thought God wanted me to give this food away, and I asked this woman if she knew anyone who needed it. Do you?"

I could feel the tears of gratitude welling up inside. Just then Amiyah came to the door, looked at the woman, and said, "Good morning, Auntie."

"Oh!" the woman said. "You have a young child. I was going to buy some toys, but I put them back. I'm so sorry. Can I give you some cash instead?"

She left soon after, and all I could do was gather Amiyah to me and fall to my knees in thanks. The food held us over until John got paid, but the lesson of how we could trust God lasted far, far longer.

†

Even though Malaysia is a Muslim nation, Christianity is tolerated there—officially, at least. So we were able to find a church nearby and join a midweek small group. At the first meeting, we saw God intervene in one of the most dramatic ways yet.

The group was made up of ten people who were all new to the church. Most were from Malaysia, but one couple, Paul and his wife, Emma, had arrived not long ago from England. We sat around the small but neat apartment and shared our stories by way of introduction. They explained that they had come to Malaysia to work with a Christian nonprofit.

I was glad John spoke for us—I was still nervous that people would find out about my dark past and reject us. But John condensed our complicated story into a few sentences, explaining a little about life on the run in Pakistan and the birth of our daughter. I listened with my eyes closed, hoping nobody would ask whether I was an ex-terrorist.

When John finished speaking, I looked up. Paul was staring at me, openmouthed.

"I know about you," he said.

I felt an unwelcome tightness return to my throat.

It seemed to me that the entire room had stopped breathing. Though I stared at the floor, I knew all eyes were on me.

Paul went on. "I was in Pakistan a year ago, meeting with some church leaders in your city. They told me about a woman on the run whose father had hung posters around the city. I'd wanted to meet you, but it wasn't possible, so we prayed for you instead."

The room was filled with silence.

Instead of fearing that I was about to be found out, I found myself overwhelmed with gratitude. God had brought us so far already. And he was with us still.

†

God's provision came in so many different ways, but there was a common thread running through each experience. In every trial and struggle was an invitation for us to learn as a family how to trust him.

One of those trials came about two years after we moved to Malaysia. The patient John was caring for died, and we found ourselves looking for a new job and a new place to live.

The only place we could afford was an apartment that had been vacant for years. It was covered in dust, filth, and strange decorations.

"Why are there so many mirrors everywhere?" John asked when we were moving in.

"They were supposed to get rid of the evil spirits," the owner said. "But it didn't work."

We felt a little strange about the dark history of our new home, but we had no choice. After a day of cleaning, the apartment looked much better. Yet while the dust and filth were gone, we woke up one night to the sound of a disturbance in the kitchen. We rushed in to find that no one was there, but all our pots and pans were on the floor.

A few days later, Amiyah got sick. Soon John and I started to feel ill too, and we knew it was time to start praying more. The three of us started each day in prayer, then prayed again in the afternoon and the evening, asking God to fill the house with his Spirit and dispel all evil. We all got healthy again, and we were reminded that nothing is more powerful than our God.

†

One night Amiyah woke up in pain. There was a thin, bloody wound running all around her neck, and ants were crawling all over her. We took her to the doctor immediately.

After the doctor treated the wounds, she had some questions for us. "Where has she been sleeping?"

"On a mat on the floor," I said.

The doctor was horrified. "You don't have a bed?" she asked. "You need to get a bed right away."

I thanked her for her time and went home, desperate once again. We barely had enough money for rent and food, let alone furniture. The only way we'd be able to get a bed would be if God provided one directly.

The next day when I was in my bedroom alone, I cried out to God, begging him to take care of our precious daughter. Then I went about my day, doing laundry and getting dinner ready. I assumed I would have to wait awhile before he acted, but that very afternoon, I met a woman who was emigrating to the United States.

"Are you from India?" the woman asked.

"No, Pakistan."

"Are you a Muslim?"

I told her I was a Christian and explained a little about why we had left Pakistan.

"Oh," she said, pausing for a moment. "Do you have a bed?"

I was taken aback. "No," I stammered.

"Can I come and visit your house?"

"Sure. We can take tea together."

We walked up the stairs, and I showed her inside. "Please," I said as she looked around, "you can sit on the mat. I'm sorry I don't have anything else for you to sit on."

The woman sat while I went to make tea. When I returned, she was crying.

"I have all these things I don't need—furniture, a washing machine, a refrigerator—and I'm going to send everything over here."

"Oh, no, Sister." I was amazed by her offer, but I didn't want to take advantage of her. "Please, I just need a bed for my little girl."

"No," she said. "I'm sending it all."

"But I can't pay."

"You don't have to pay. I'm giving it all to you."

I watched with tears in my eyes as two men filled our house

with everything she'd described, as well as a TV, fans, and a table. The whole apartment was filled instantly.

When John returned later that day, he looked around our home in shock. "Where did all this come from?"

I explained the whole story, but John was upset. "Do you think I'm a beggar? I told you to give me some time to work and save, and we'd get what we need slowly."

"But I didn't ask anyone for anything. She just saw how little we had and sent it all over."

"Then call her and tell her to take it back."

"But this is God's gift, John. And if he's given it to us, how can we refuse him?"

John was crying now. "I am not a beggar."

He went upstairs to take a shower, and I called Paul from our small group. He and John had formed a strong friendship, and I knew that if there was anyone who could talk to John, it was Paul.

He arrived at our home within an hour. "Wow!" Paul stood in the middle of the apartment, an arm around John and a wide smile across his face. "Praise God! Your house is full of blessings!"

John stared around him, seeing the gifts in a new light. "You're right," he said. "It is."

"You have everything now," Paul said. "I was going to encourage the church to help you get all this furniture month by month, but God works this way sometimes. And his timing is always perfect, isn't it?"

John nodded. By now his smile was almost as wide as Paul's.

Paul was right: God had provided everything we needed. Even here, so far from home, God was reminding us just how close he was.

28

"No, God," I said. "Please, not that."

We had been in Malaysia for five years. We'd been granted refugee status and had applied to be resettled elsewhere as refugees. Now we were just waiting for the United Nations to give us our final settlement location. John had found a job with a nonprofit, I was homeschooling our daughter, and our family felt loved, accepted, and embraced by our church. Everything was going as well as it could, considering we were far from our families.

Ever since I had become a Christian, I tried to pray more than I did as a Muslim, so I began waking at three o'clock every morning to pray for an hour. One time, when the house was silent apart from my whispered prayers, God spoke. *You need to share everything I've done in your life.*

I knew what that would require. In order to talk about God's rescue, I would have to explain how far away from him

I had been. I would have to reveal the secret I had kept hidden deep within me since the night I said good-bye to my mother and crept out of the house.

"Everything? But John will leave me if he finds out I was plotting to kill Christians," I begged.

I am with you.

I heard nothing else after that.

I knew the Lord was right—how could I hide the transformation he'd done in my life? And I knew whom I needed to tell first.

"John," I said later that day, after he had finished eating his favorite meal of fried fish and chapatti. "I want to share something with you. Please don't be angry."

He shot me a worried look and put his hand on mine. "It's okay. If anything happened, you can tell me."

"You promise you won't divorce me?"

"What happened?"

"I want you to promise," I said, unable to stop myself from crying. "If you leave me, I'll have nowhere to go and no one to go to. And I can't go back."

"Esther, I'm not going to leave you. Even if something bad has happened, I won't leave you. Even if it's something like adultery. Mistakes can happen to anyone."

I took a breath and tried to find my voice again. "There's one part of my life that I've kept hidden from everyone, but it has always been open to God. I want to tell you who I was before we met. Do you remember the first church we visited here, when the pastor asked if I was an ex-terrorist?"

"Yes," John said. "That made me so angry."

"He was right."

John stared at me, confused.

I told him everything. When I was finished, he asked me

why I had never told him about the madrassa, the call for jihad, and the day I raised my hand.

"I hoped God wouldn't reveal it," I whispered.

He was quiet for a while.

As the silence between us stretched out, I feared that he might respond the way my father so often did—by rejecting me and withdrawing his love. Surely this would finally be too much for John. He had given up so much for me, but how much more could he be expected to sacrifice? Could I really expect him to accept the fact that I had been so ready to embrace evil?

When he finally spoke, his words were slow and heavy but filled with warmth. "It's okay. This is your past. I know how much you love God now."

"Yes," I said. "You know that from the first drop of blood to the last, my life is for the Lord."

We talked a little more, and while the news had come as a shock to him, John was able to forgive me and accept what I'd told him.

"The only thing I'm worried about is telling other people," he said. "Maybe it's better to keep the truth between us and God. Other people might not understand."

"I see what you're saying," I said as we sat on the bed. "But I can't keep quiet anymore. God has told me to tell people, so I have to speak."

†

John had reason to fear how people would react when I told my story. While being a Christian in a Muslim nation like Malaysia was nowhere near as dangerous as it was in Pakistan, we were still an unwelcome minority. There were plenty of Muslims in Malaysia who reacted to Christians with anger and abuse.

Early on during our time there, I was waiting at a bus stop with Amiyah when a woman in a hijab started talking to her. Amiyah was three and a half, with curly hair, chubby cheeks, and fair skin, and the woman gently rubbed her back and told me in Malay that she thought my daughter was beautiful.

"Thank you," I said in English.

"Are you Malaysian?" she asked.

"No, I'm from Pakistan."

"Ah," she nodded. "Islam?"

"No." I made a cross with my two index fingers. "Christian."

The woman's face soured. She still had her hand on Amiyah's back and pushed her hard. Amiyah fell forward and hit her face on the ground. I picked her up and saw that blood was pouring from her mouth. Thankfully it was just her lip, but I squeezed her tight to me, desperate to take away the pain.

When she calmed down a little, I looked Amiyah in the eye. "It's okay," I said. "When we're Christians, people will do this to us. We can forgive them just as Jesus has forgiven us."

It hurt to see my daughter facing persecution at such a young age, but how could I shield her completely from the rejection we will all face as followers of Jesus? And if I was really honest with myself, did I even want to? More than a life free from opposition, I wanted my daughter to know that in the face of hatred she could learn the way of Jesus—the way of love and grace and forgiveness.

†

Our apartment had lots of windows but no air-conditioning, which meant that every afternoon the air inside grew so hot and stale it was impossible to concentrate on schoolwork. On especially hot days, we would take our books outside and I'd homeschool Amiyah right on the playground equipment.

While she studied, I would talk with other moms and tell them about how my life had changed since my dream about Jesus.

It was not easy, and I was surprised by how much harder it was to introduce strangers to Jesus than it had been to talk to my mother, sister, and brother. Some of the women I met at the playground were interested in what I had to tell them, but for every open opportunity, there were many more conversations that ended with hard stares and turned backs.

Sometimes the discouragement got to me. There was one period when John was without work and the cupboards were bare and I missed home, and it hurt when I talked about Jesus and people spat insults in return. I could feel the weight of all the rejection that had built up in the decade since I became a Christian.

It was as if I were a child again. I needed to know that God hadn't left me, that he still cared about my family and me. I decided to fast and pray, and after three days, I finally heard his gentle whisper. *Daughter, my Spirit, who brought you from Pakistan, is still with you. In your painful times and in your joyful times, I am still with you.*

I wept. "I'm so sorry," I whispered.

My work for you in Malaysia continues. But when you're done here, nothing will stop you from what I have in store for you next.

"Please, Lord," I begged, "give me the work you have called me to!"

The next day a friend introduced me to a Muslim family that was applying to be resettled as refugees and needed advice. I visited them at the same asylum center we had stayed in when we arrived.

"Thank you for being so kind and coming to us," the wife said as we waited for her husband to join us. "But tell me, why don't you come to Islam? Allah's mercy should be on you."

I smiled, remembering how I, too, had learned the three-step plan to convert a Christian.

"I'm already under mercy," I said. "What do you think about becoming a Christian?"

"No." She frowned. "Their book has been changed."

"Really? Who changed it?"

"I don't know," she said.

"Well, when you find out who changed it and when, you should shout it out. But until then, I don't think you should spread rumors. Christians are kind and loving, and Jesus is still performing miracles today."

This made her think. "Have you seen any miracles?"

"Yes—many," I said.

She paused. "Okay, I want you to pray for me. I want to know if you're right and Jesus really can heal me."

She was a diabetic and took insulin, and I prayed for her before her husband joined us.

A month later, this woman called me. She'd just had a checkup, and her blood sugar levels were normal. Her doctor had taken her off insulin.

I visited her again soon after, and we talked about how Jesus still heals today, just as he did in the Holy Bible. I asked her why she didn't read the Bible when it contained three of the holy books that all Muslims are supposed to read, and she said she didn't really know why.

We talked more, and our conversations reminded me of the debates. She was an educated woman, and I encouraged her to think deeply, to look carefully at the Qur'an, and to ask questions.

I visited her regularly for three months, and during that time the whole family became Christians. They found a local church that embraced and nurtured them, and soon after, we heard that the United Nations had accepted their appeal. Within months they left Malaysia, ready to start a new life in Europe.

This was a bittersweet victory for us. We were thrilled for our friends, but their departure was also a reminder of how delayed our own process was. We were approaching our seventh year in Malaysia, and so far every stage of our application had taken longer than any other case we'd heard of. Where others had to wait weeks for an appointment, we waited months. When we were told to expect a response in months, we knew it could take years. We tried to find out why, but we never received any official explanation.

In the midst of the waiting, we learned yet another valuable lesson. Whenever we compared our situation to that of others, we would get upset. There was always someone with a smoother application process, better accommodations, or fewer obstacles. But whenever we reminded ourselves of what Jesus went through—from his lowly birth to his agonizing death—we looked at our own circumstances with fresh eyes. What we faced was nothing compared to what the Son of God, who traded the glory of heaven for the pain of the cross, endured. Remembering that helped us to persevere. This perspective reminded us to remain faithful, because we were convinced that when the Lord wanted us out of Malaysia, nothing could stop him.

†

I continued sharing about Christ with moms at the playground, taxi drivers, friends of friends, and anyone else I came into contact with. I started seeing more people come to faith, and these victories gave me profound encouragement. The more I shared and the more I prayed, the more I learned to search for the lesson God was teaching in every situation.

One day as I was waiting for a bus with Amiyah, who was about eight at the time, a man approached. He had a long beard and the traditional white cotton robes of a devoted Muslim. I had a sense from the start that this was not going to end well.

"I want to sit there," he said, pointing at the bench where Amiyah was sitting.

I told her in English to come and sit on my lap.

"You are Malaysian?" he asked.

"No, I'm from Pakistan."

"Oh! Pakistan," he said, nodding. "Islam?"

"No." I shook my head and smiled. "Christian."

He stared at me for a second, not flinching. Then he threw back his head and spat at me. He missed me but hit Amiyah squarely in the face. She started crying, but the man raged on.

"Why are you Christians here in our country? Get out of here. I don't like Christians. If I were the prime minister, I . . ."

I stopped listening. I was trying to calm Amiyah down. When our bus came, the man didn't move. I looked at him, said thank you, and got on the bus with Amiyah.

Later that evening, she told John all about it. He knelt down in front of her, listening carefully. When she was done crying, he took her hands in his and spoke quietly. "The same thing happened to Jesus. They spit on him, beat him, and hurt him. But nothing could change his mind about loving people the way God wanted him to."

"Why?" Amiyah asked.

John opened his Bible, and together they read about Jesus being beaten and crucified.

"You know," he said, "I think it does us good to feel some of the pain he endured before he was crucified."

Even as I ached for my daughter, I felt gratitude wash over me. She would not be immune to pain as a Christian, but she had a father who loved her and accepted her—and who showed her what the heavenly Father's love is like.

29

God chose a remarkable man to be my husband. It took several years after we were married for me to understand just how remarkable.

The longer we stayed in Malaysia, the more grateful I became for John's faith. He was unshakable. Whenever I felt weary of all the waiting or became fearful that we might get sent back home, John remained steady. He never failed to remind me of all God had done, and he helped me take my focus off my worries and retrain my eyes on Jesus.

What's more, John felt confident about where we were headed.

There had been two occasions in his life when God had revealed to John certain insights about what lay ahead. The first was when he was fourteen. He felt sure that God was calling him to convert one person and encouraging him that he would one day get married. The details were unclear to him, and he didn't believe that there would be any connection between the person he converted and the person he married. But this quickly became a passion he carried with him for years: to win one soul for the Lord and to find the person God would have him marry.

Before John and I met, he had another dream that was so detailed and vibrant he never forgot it. He saw his life years into the future. He was working in a medical lab, enduring periods of great suffering, before moving to a new apartment in an unknown country and then finally relocating to a different country overseas.

When I stood in his lab and told him I didn't think I was a Muslim any longer, John knew the first part of God's plan was in motion—that I was the one he had been called to convert. And when we walked through the half-empty airport in Pakistan and were waved through by the sleepy-looking border guards, he knew that the second part was under way as well. The day we saw our first apartment in Malaysia, John knew the rest of the plan was in place. It was the exact same apartment he had seen in his dream—the same walls, the same windows, the same feel. John knew God was directing us exactly where he wanted us to be. He knew that the final bit of his dream would one day come true: we would all move to America.

†

Without a divine plan in place, it didn't make sense to believe that any Western country would accept us as refugees, let alone the United States. My past was so complicated and there were so many other refugees who wanted entry into the States—how could we even dare to dream of leaving Malaysia and starting a new life there?

But we knew God had spoken, and we knew we could trust him.

So that's exactly what we did: we chose to trust God in all circumstances. When we had to spend eight hours waiting in the blistering heat in Kuala Lumpur to find out whether our paperwork had been processed, we trusted that God was in control. When people who had arrived in Malaysia long after we did were informed that they'd been offered a new life as refugees in Europe, we resisted the fear that God had abandoned us. And when we were given reason to suspect that our application in Malaysia was being deliberately delayed, we remained determined to keep faith in God.

After a long process, we were finally granted refugee status, which enabled us to approach the UNHCR, the UN refugee agency. They would help us find a country to be our new home. A worker explained the first choice we had to make: we could either apply to one country or submit an open application to all the countries the UNHCR worked with and take whichever country chose us.

We knew God was sending us to America, but we wanted to give him control, so we opted for the second choice. After almost eight years of waiting, we were told that out of all the possible countries—from Canada to Australia to Denmark to New Zealand to a host of others—our application had been selected by the one country we'd been hoping for. We were going to America.

But not yet. We found ourselves at the beginning of yet another slow-moving leg of our journey. John and I were interviewed at length about our past in Pakistan, and as we'd done when we first arrived in Malaysia, we had to wait many months between the interviews and the applications. Our case was reviewed so many times that I began to wonder whether it would ever come to an end. But no matter how bleak things looked, John was always able to remind me of the hope we had in Jesus.

One night when I was praying in my room, I felt like God had left me. I'd been to the UNHCR the day before to check on our case, and when I was finally called up to talk with one of the Malaysian staff members, things had not gone well.

"You want to talk?" she asked, her arms folded in front of her. I saw that my file was unopened on her desk. "I'm listening."

"Please," I said, trying to keep my voice calm. "My daughter needs to go to school, and we need help."

"Help? Why should we help you? We didn't invite you here. We didn't say we'd help, and we're not here to educate your children. Stop disturbing us. Go home. We'll call you if we need you."

It was not the first time I had been treated rudely, and it certainly was not the worst. All the same, the incident troubled me—not because of what the woman had said but because of what I had seen. Written in bold letters across my file were these words: "Woman converted from Islam to Christianity."

As I prayed, my face was covered in tears and my throat was raw. I wanted to wake John and have him tell me for the thousandth time why everything was going to be just fine, but he had to work the next day, and I knew he needed to sleep.

As I told God how big the problems were and how powerless I felt and how desperate it all looked, I felt weaker than ever. My mind spun back to the time John and I had stood in front of his pastor, begging him to marry us. I had reminded the pastor of the parable of the lost sheep, repeating to him words that John had said to me many times.

I was no longer a lost sheep. I had been found by God,

brought into the fold. I was a Christian. I belonged. And yet I was still weak. I still needed rescuing.

It wasn't a dramatic moment, and I didn't hear God's audible voice in the darkness. But that night something changed within me. I was reminded of my weakness and my dependence on God. That night, yet again, I surrendered everything to him.

†

While I had spent much of our time in Malaysia worrying about how we would get out, John's prayers were usually focused on the people who had looked after us during the two years we were on the run in Pakistan. His heart was broken for them as they faced poverty and persecution, and even though we often struggled to afford to buy food for ourselves, he always made sure we sent them money whenever we could.

The longer we were married, the more I realized how much John and I had in common. His father had died when John was the same age I had been when I left home. His mother was dead now too, and he had not been able to make contact with anyone in his family since we fled the city. My parents might not have been dead, but for all practical purposes, they were dead to me. I couldn't even risk a phone call to check on my mother's health, knowing that even if I called from a pay phone, my father would see the country code and come after me and my family. I could not risk putting Amiyah in danger like that.

In many ways, John had lost even more than I had. He had voluntarily left his family and church and community behind for my sake, but I never heard him complain or waver. Whenever I asked him what I had done to deserve such a wonderful husband, he would just smile and wave his hand in the air.

"God has given me this heart," he'd say. "I am with you."

30

The morning we dragged our seven suitcases through the gates of the UNHCR compound, I was so nervous that I thought I would explode. With every passing minute, I felt my insides twist tighter and tighter. I had good reason to be worried. It was the day we were flying out of Malaysia for the United States, and in one of our suitcases were my notes about the Qur'an. Over the years, I had written hundreds of notes based on my research of the Qur'an and the Bible. If these papers were spotted by an eager customs official at the airport, there was a chance I could be charged with blasphemy. If that happened, I would be right back where I started ten years earlier.

Amiyah was nervous too, but more out of excitement than fear. "Where are they taking our bags?" "Are you sure these windows don't open?" "How will the plane know when to land?" Answering her questions was a welcome distraction for me.

I made it safely through customs with my Qur'an, but once we were airborne, my insides still refused to relax. It gradually dawned on me that my worries were about more than my defaced copy of the Qur'an. For the previous eight years, I'd held tightly to the belief that America was where God wanted us in the next phase of our lives. Now that we were hurtling there at five hundred miles per hour, I realized I had absolutely no idea what this new life in the States would look like. Besides the fact that we would have a caseworker, a rented house, and some financial assistance until John and I found jobs, everything that lay ahead of us was a question mark.

Just two weeks earlier we had learned where we were going to be living, and until that moment neither of us had ever heard of the state, let alone the city. We looked at each other, wide eyed, not even sure which part of the map to look at.

I was reminded of Hebrews 11:8: "It was by faith that Abraham obeyed when God called him to leave home and go to another land that God would give him as his inheritance. He went without knowing where he was going" (NLT). We didn't know where we were going. But God did. And I had been through enough with God to know that trusting him does not always mean feeling calm and reassured. I had learned that sometimes I just had to take the leap in the midst of my fear, knowing my Father would catch me before I landed.

Amiyah, on the other hand, was now a picture of perfect trust. She watched movies throughout the flight, and John slept much of the way. I spent most of the time staring at the map on the screen in front of me, watching the tiny plane inch its way across the ocean. It was good to be reminded that wherever we were heading and whatever this new life held for us, God was in control. I could see only what the map revealed, but God knew every inch of land and every drop of ocean between here and there. Nothing was hidden from him.

†

Ultimately it took us two years to leave Pakistan and eight years to leave Malaysia but only two days to feel at home in America. On the first day and night, we were tired and disoriented, shocked by how much quieter our neighborhood was than Kuala Lumpur had been. Perhaps most of all, we were unsure of what the coming days would hold. Two of our suitcases, including the one with the Qur'an, had gone missing, which added to the sense of unease we felt. We had no way of knowing if someone had intentionally confiscated it or if it was an incidental loss.

But when we woke up the next day and realized it was Sunday, we knew exactly what we needed to do. We needed to go to church.

We spent the day among strangers who instantly became friends. Many of these new brothers and sisters had never met anyone from Pakistan before, and we had never been to a church that felt so relaxed and open before, yet we prayed and worshiped as one. We laughed, talked, and shared stories, and afterward our new friends invited us to eat with them. By the time we returned home, full of gratitude, great food, and praise, we knew that we belonged.

†

We arrived in the United States in the height of summer, but as the leaves started to turn brown and the days grew shorter, we were feeling settled in our new life. Amiyah was getting straight As in school, and John had found work at a local health clinic. When they both were out during the day, I only had to look around the house to be reminded of God's provision and the wonderful generosity of the church. That first weekend, the house had been almost empty, but within months it was stocked with everything we needed, from closets full of clothes to a washer and dryer, and even a car to drive.

Despite this provision, I would often fall to my knees, desperate for God to help us. John's wages were small, but large enough to reduce the amount of financial assistance we received from the state. People from church continued to donate items we needed, but at times there simply was not enough money to pay the bills. Over the time we had spent in Malaysia, we gradually felt less and less like refugees. We belonged to our church community, we had work and a little money, and we looked like everyone else in the country. In the States, we were starting over as refugees, and it took time to readjust.

The financial challenges were not the only pressures we felt. Back in Malaysia, Amiyah had started to ask questions about her grandparents, and we always tried to give her answers she'd be able to understand. But by the time we moved to the United States, she was ten and able to comprehend much of the story about how her mom and dad had met. Knowing that she had a grandmother and a grandfather on my side, as well as uncles and aunts and cousins she had never met, left Amiyah feeling sad. She would see her friends at school getting picked up by their relatives or hear about her classmates spending time with their extended families over the weekend, and she'd feel a deep sense of loss. She had never met any of her relatives, but she missed them all the same.

Some pressures we kept from Amiyah. One day I returned home after walking her to school on Martin Luther King Day and found a note from the KKK attached to a rock, telling all foreigners to get out of the neighborhood. I called a friend from church immediately, and she put in a call to the police.

"They do this every year," the officer told her. "It's nothing personal."

John and I chose to trust the advice and ignore the note. Months passed, and there were no more threats. But when we heard gunshots in the street outside one spring night, I felt the fear return to my throat. Even though we knew the gunshots belonged to another person's quarrel, I did not sleep well that night.

†

There was a time when *jihad* was one of the most important words I knew. It takes many forms, but all expressions of jihad share the common theme of struggle. For some people, jihad is about struggling against poverty; for others, like my former self, it's a struggle against those we believed to be the enemies of Islam. My whole life was a struggle, even though I couldn't always see that.

In many ways, my life as a Muslim was defined by the struggles I faced. I struggled to get love from my father. I tried so hard, working to the best of my ability at school just to get his attention. But the struggle was futile. He had no interest in his third-born daughter.

I struggled for the right to receive an education. My father put many restrictions on me, but I fought to get as much instruction as possible. Even though I felt like I was winning that battle, I had no peace inside. I desperately wanted acceptance and love, and those were things even the best teachers could not give me.

So I had done the only thing I knew how to do in my

limited human understanding: I prepared to struggle against the infidels.

All my struggles didn't go away the day I dreamed of Jesus. In many ways, that was the beginning of a new struggle. As a Christian, I had to struggle to prove to myself and my community that my decision to leave Islam was right. Then I struggled to keep myself, my husband, and my daughter safe.

We struggled in Malaysia, too. We had to make a fresh start, knowing no one and with nothing but a few dollars in our pockets. I struggled to put aside my fear and doubt and choose to trust my God and share my full story with others.

There has been so much struggle.

But the difference between the way I struggled as a Muslim and the way I struggle as a Christian is significant. Today I don't struggle alone. God doesn't stand apart from me, keeping a record of my sins so he can weigh them against my good deeds and then use my sins to keep me from him. Instead, my God reveals his true nature through his Son, Jesus. Christ stands with arms stretched open, broken and bloodied, scarred and suffering. He has struggled far more than I ever will. And no matter what struggle I face, I won't face it alone. He will be right by my side.

Perhaps most freeing of all, it's not up to us to earn our own salvation. God gives us his grace and love—the most powerful force in the world. That means I no longer have to struggle to be accepted. Jihad was all about what I could do; salvation is about what God has done for me—for all of us.

31

"You were *a Muslim?"*

I paused the sewing machine and looked around. The workshop was small—not much bigger than my mother's workshop back in Pakistan. Even though I knew I was safe and that a conversation like this in the United States was no more controversial than a discussion about politics, I still felt nervous.

I'd been working at the sewing shop for three days, sitting at the bench alongside four other women as we made costumes for an upcoming city parade. The bright fabrics reminded me of home, as did the women's laughter as they teased the delivery guy who hovered nervously in the doorway. Happy memories from a lifetime ago came flooding through my mind.

"What do you mean, you used to be a Muslim? I don't understand." Nasirah was looking at me intently. She was the only Muslim in the workshop—at least, she was the only woman wearing a veil—and from the moment I met her, I had been praying for an opportunity to talk to her about Jesus. Even so, it still felt like a risk to say, "Yes. I was born and raised a Muslim." Would she see me as a kafir? What if she had ties to militants? I watched her search my face as she realized that I was not who she thought I was.

I knew I needed to tell her more. "Something happened to me," I said, determined to make the most of this opportunity. "Something I never expected—but it opened my eyes to the truth."

I noticed the twitch in her mouth, the narrowing of her eyes. I was no longer a target for friendly evangelism but an infidel worthy of scorn. I knew I didn't have long before she dismissed me and shut down the conversation, so I kept talking, telling Nasirah my story in a handful of sentences. To my surprise, she didn't interrupt me or turn away. She just listened, her eyes locked on the wisp of bright red thread in her hands. As we talked, I prayed silently, asking God to breathe life into my words and ignite a hunger within Nasirah to know more about him.

When I was done telling my story, I didn't know what else to say, so I extended an invitation. "Would you like to come to my home to talk some more?"

"Yes," she said, looking up at me. "I'd like that."

†

It took me a while to adjust to the freedom of life in the United States. Being able to work, drive, use public transportation without fear of strangers—all these experiences are so different from what we faced as Christians in Pakistan and Malaysia.

Other changes have been more difficult to come to terms

with. Ever since I left home, I've been moving farther and farther away from my family. I know it is unlikely that I will ever see them or even have contact with them again. I don't know if my mother is still alive. I may never know if my father and my two older sisters came to Christ. Amiyah will never know her grandparents or her aunts and uncles and cousins. It has been more than ten years since I left my family, but the risk is still too great—if my father is the man he used to be, nothing will stop him from killing my family and me for the sake of his religion and his honor.

But even in the face of those losses, God has provided. We have been blessed with so many friends here, and one family in particular has adopted our family into theirs. I might never reconnect with my family in Pakistan, but I know I'll always have a mom and a sister here in the United States who will love me, care for me, and protect me.

I am so glad Amiyah will grow up in a country like this, where she is free to learn and live as God calls her to live. But the temptations of the world are great, and John and I know that, like all Christian families in the West, we can't take for granted that our daughter will continue to grow in the Lord. Children need to be taught and shown how great our God is and how important he is in our lives. We have to pray together and read the Bible together as a family. Like every child, our daughter needs to be equipped. She may never debate a mullah or face a roomful of angry militants, but she still must be ready—ready to take risks for God, ready to trust him no matter what.

†

Of all the changes in my life since I've come to the States, the most significant has been the freedom to share my story freely in public. Ever since I moved here, I've known that I can't stay silent. What God has done in my life is something I cannot hide. The days of keeping my past to myself are behind me.

So wherever and whenever I can, I share my story. I speak up at work, and I speak up in the grocery store. I talk to Muslims from all around the world on Facebook, and I speak in churches in my area. Sometimes I talk with a crowd of a hundred; other times I sit and talk with one person. It doesn't matter how many or how few are there—all that matters is that I share what God has done.

As I talk to people, I am aware that while my story is different from other people's, in many ways it isn't unique at all. God is powerfully at work in the lives of Muslims today, and over the last couple of decades millions have come to faith in him. Like me, many met him in dreams. Others met him through evangelism and outreach, whether in their own country or in the West.

As the local church, we have the joy and the responsibility of inviting these individuals with Muslim backgrounds into the family of God. Our world is growing increasingly small, and when people come from other countries or from other religions, my hope is that the church will accept them with love and joy. After all, God loved these people enough to cross boundaries and borders to bring them home, and we have the privilege of doing the same.

They need our help—financially, emotionally, physically. There are so many ways in which we can share the burden of someone who has to leave everything behind so that they can follow God. He invites all of us to play our parts, whether that means sharing our faith with a skeptic at school or work like Azia and John did for me, opening our homes for displaced believers as many Christians did for us in Pakistan, or spending years walking alongside new Christians as Paul and C. Howe did for us in Malaysia. Whatever our resources, whatever our situations, whatever our gifts, God invites each of us to join the work he is doing.

So if you happen to meet a refugee or a family of refugees, don't rush away out of fear or uncertainty over what to say and do. Ask God how he is inviting you to be involved. How can you help? What part can you play? What would God have you do to reveal a little more of his love to them? Ask them what they need too. Ask them about their stories, and share your story too.

As you listen, you might discover that their journey has been full of struggles and sorrow, pain and persecution. It might be different from yours in dramatic ways, but there will be similarities, too. For isn't it just like God to bring different people together? Isn't it just like God to weave strength out of brokenness in all of us? Isn't it just like him to use the unqualified and the weak to be a part of his plan?

My life started with a wound. It festered, making me ever more desperate for the love and attention of a father who was determined to turn his face from me. But God was there. He saw my hurt, and he saw all the foolish ways I tried to mask the pain. And when I was about to make the gravest mistake of my life, he stepped in and rescued me.

I will never know how many lives God saved when he took me off the path of jihad. Perhaps I'll never know whether God has rescued my father, my sisters, and people like Anwar. But I know for sure that none of us are too far from God's hand. All of us are invited to know the love and acceptance that our perfect heavenly Father offers.

For this is the God who loves us. He takes us, wounded and weak and misguided as we are, and brings us home.

Q and A with Esther Ahmad

Are you in contact with anyone from back home in Pakistan?
I am not in touch with my family at all, and that breaks my heart. Amiyah often notices other children with their grandparents, and it makes both of us sad to realize she'll never know her grandparents and the rest of her extended family.

Today we are in touch with John's family, as well as his pastor, his church community, and many of the people who helped us when we were on the run. These believers continue to face persecution in Pakistan and live under the threat of violence. One of John's brothers has been beaten, and other Christians who helped us have been attacked. A piece of our hearts will always be in Pakistan.

How do you handle not being able to communicate with your family, especially your mother and your siblings?
At times it has been really difficult to cope. Even today, it is still painful. When we first arrived in Malaysia, I would wake up every morning while Amiyah was asleep and cry. One day, when John came back early from work, he found me in tears. He asked me why I was crying, and I told him that I was missing my family.

"How long have you been crying?" he asked, putting his arm around me.

I told him that I had spent the last three hours in tears.

"And did your parents come back? Did crying change anything?"

"No."

"Why spend so long crying every day if you get nothing out of it? Why not spend those hours in prayer for them? Pray for your mother's faith to grow strong in Christ Jesus, and pray for the power to forgive your father. In this way, you will get peace in your heart and mind."

Starting the next day, that is exactly what I did. I felt comforted right away. Even now I begin every day praying for my family. That is how I cope.

What do you miss about your homeland, particularly knowing you'll likely never return?

I miss my family, my Christian friends, and the fellowship we shared. All the people who looked after us while we were on the run became like family to me. They walked the extra mile with us, just as Jesus tells us to do. We have been able to keep in touch with some of them and send them money when we can, as they are still facing persecution.

I miss seeing the beautiful places in Pakistan, such as the northern mountains around Murree and the beautiful valleys of Kalash and Kaghan. I do not miss Pakistani food though—I can cook that pretty well at home! Chapattis, biriyani, and chicken masala are all regular dishes on our table.

Some things about American life still seem strange to us: days when the sun stays behind heavy clouds, times when I am alone at home. The most confusing thing is that even though people here are well and blessed and could go to church without any restrictions, they do not. When I was in Pakistan and I could not go to church, I would daydream about how wonderful it would be to be able to worship with God's people. I thought that the Christians in the United States would be so happy to be able to go to church whenever they wanted to, but instead they want to go to the beach, watch football, or eat. It makes me a bit sad.

What are the biggest adjustments your family has faced as you are living in an unfamiliar culture?

Being a refugee in the United States has not been a bad experience for us. The government has helped us with jobs and finding work, and our church and local community have played a big part in making our transition easier. We arrived without two of our bags, so John and I had to wear the same clothes for three days. But the pastor of the first church we went to jumped in to help. He and some other people from the church took us shopping and bought us what we needed. Other people from the congregation invited us to eat with them and helped us in so many different ways. Someone even gave us a car! Their generosity was truly remarkable.

When we were in Malaysia, we were surrounded by people from so many different countries, so some parts of American culture are a little familiar to us. One of the challenges we didn't expect was all the confusing paperwork! Perhaps the biggest adjustment is that John's work qualifications and experience do not count over here, so he has to start his studies all over again if he wants to get a job in the same profession.

Amiyah has faced a few difficulties with other pupils at school, but she has handled them with courage, love, and prayer. I can see how God is using her already!

In what ways have you been welcomed in your new home?

We have been helped by so many wonderful people in local churches. They have given practical help and support—furniture, clothes, food—and they have invited us to become part of their families. At a point when I was particularly missing my mom, and Amiyah was sad that she does not know her aunties or grandmother, God sent us Lisa, a woman we met at church. Early on she said to me, "Call me Mom" and to Amiyah, "Call me Gran," and there has not been a day when I have not thanked God for her.

God has gone before us in so many ways and has provided us with such a loving, generous bunch of people. We are eternally grateful for family in the form of our Christian brothers and sisters here.

What misconceptions would you say people have about Muslims?

It's common for people in the West to assume that all Muslims spread hate and support terrorism. Even though I was prepared to give my life for jihad, I don't believe that all Muslims feel this way. I was part of a dangerous minority, but in my opinion, there are many good, sensible, and educated Muslims out there who reject the jihad ideology mentioned in the Qur'an.

Do Christians and Muslims worship the same God?

When I was a Muslim, I believed that, yes, Muslims and Christians worship the same God. As a Christian, I no longer believe that. From all my experience—through my study of the Bible and the Qur'an, prayer, and everything that happened to me in Pakistan—I can say that the differences between the God of the Bible and Allah are so vast that they simply cannot be the same God. God is merciful and loving, but Allah has no mercy and no love.

In observing your debates about the Qur'an and the Bible, someone could say that the Bible's inerrancy could be picked apart the way you challenged the Qur'an. How would you respond to that?

At its core, the Bible is built on truth. It points us to Jesus and invites us to deepen our own relationship with God. The Qur'an is built on confusion. Muslims are not encouraged to wrestle with it or to search for the truth themselves, and it is filled with contradictions. With the story of Jonah, for example, the account of how long he spent in the belly of the big fish varies throughout the Qur'an and the hadith: in some places it says one day, in others it says three, seven, or forty. That is why Muslims are not encouraged to read the Qur'an in their native tongue or question it in any way. I love the way we Christians can engage with and debate about the Bible—it is strong enough to withstand our questions. And searching for truth is exactly what we are encouraged to do. In Luke 11:9, Jesus says, "Ask and it will be given to you; seek and you will find; knock and the door will be opened to you."

How does the church in the United States compare to the church in Pakistan?

Churches in the United States are different from churches in Pakistan. Though people in the United States are materially blessed and have more opportunities, many don't like to go to church. Pastors here are more focused on serving the church community and encouraging more people to attend.

In Pakistan, the Christians struggle. They attend church passionately, desperate for prayer and worship. Some churches receive bomb threats, but they keep on meeting. The pastors are often at the greatest risk.

But we have plenty in common. We all worship, read the Bible, and pray to the same God! He's big enough to know and care for us all.

What advice do you have for a Christian who wants to share about Christ with a Muslim?

Be a good Christian! As it says in the Gospel of Matthew (5:16), "Let your light shine before others, that they may see your good deeds and glorify your Father in heaven." Our greatest role model is the Lord Jesus Christ. He set the example for us to follow, so we should love, serve, and pray for people, just as he did.

It's important to remember that making disciples is not just a matter of getting people to go to one really great meeting or doing a week of fellowship with them. God can intervene and make himself known to them in a matter of moments, like he did with me, but the journey of learning to follow him takes a long, long time. If we want to share our faith with Muslims, we must be prepared to walk extra miles, to do extra work. Be a positive person in their lives, share your testimony well, and be prepared to be a good friend for as long as it takes. And pray, learning to allow God alone to direct your words and actions.

Notes

1. Qur'an 18:86.
2. Qur'an 12:31, 50.
3. Qur'an 80:1-10.
4. Qur'an 4:136.
5. *Sahih Bukhari*, "Prophetic Commentary on the Qur'an (Tafseer of the Prophet)," trans. M. Muhsin Khan, volume 6, book 60, number 300.
6. *Sahih Muslim*, "The Book of Faith (Kitab Al-Iman)," trans. Abdul Hamid Siddiqui, book 001, number 0004, chapter 2.
7. John 14:6.
8. Romans 8:31.
9. 1 Peter 3:13.
10. Matthew 5:10-12.
11. Exodus 20:12.
12. Ephesians 6:1.
13. Romans 8:18.
14. James 1:5.
15. Qur'an 10:37.
16. Qur'an 16:89.
17. Qur'an 29:27.
18. Luke 12:11-12.
19. *Sahih Muslim*, "The Book of Zakat (Kitab Al-Zakat)," volume 3, book 005, number 2263.
20. Qur'an 4:158.
21. Matthew 10:30.
22. Isaiah 49:16.
23. Qur'an 5:69.
24. See Matthew 18:12-14.

Discussion Questions

1. The author grew up feeling unloved and unwanted by her father. How did the rejection she experienced affect her?

2. What is your idea of what God is like as a heavenly Father? What has influenced this perception? (If you would like to explore what the Bible says about God as Father, here are some places to start: Matthew 7:11; Romans 8:15; 1 John 3:1.)

3. The theme of part 1 of the book is "Everyone has to die sometime"—a rather stark statement. How does contemplating your own death influence the way you live your life? What legacy would you like to leave?

4. The author fell prey to what she describes as a "militant Islamic extremist" group that characterized Westerners as infidels. Along with others in her community, she was called upon to join the fight against this enemy. Jesus said, "Love your enemies and pray for those who persecute you" (Matthew 5:44). Do you think this verse applies to both Muslims and Christians? How does it apply to you personally?

5. The author was told that if her good deeds outweighed the bad, she would go to heaven. Although she prayed more than what was required and did many good deeds, she was haunted by uncertainty, not knowing whether her efforts were enough. How does the Christian view of salvation differ from trying to earn one's way to heaven? (You may wish to consult a few of these verses: Romans 3:23-24; Ephesians 2:8-9; Titus 3:4-7.)

6. Looking back at her childhood, the author realized that violence in her home increased under the influence of the militant extremist group. She remembers her father beating her mother, exerting control through pain and fear. How does the violence promoted in this strain of Islam differ from what the Bible teaches? How is Jesus' view of women different from what the author experienced in her home?

7. The book tells of Auntie Selma's family dying for the cause of jihad and how the community considered them heroes. How do you view their deaths and their community's response to their sacrifice? What fresh insights does Esther's story give you into the mind of a would-be terrorist?

8. As a science student, the author questioned superstitions that her mother believed, causing her to begin to doubt her religion. After she converted to Christianity, she engaged in debates with Islamic scholars. What does this tell us about the role of using one's mind in seeking truth? How we can talk with people from a different faith background in a loving and respectful way?

9. Like many Muslims, the author was taught that Christianity has three major flaws: it follows three Gods; it claims that Jesus is the Son of God; and its book, the Bible, has been changed. How would you respond to these three criticisms?

10. The author had a dream, related in chapter 9, that took place in a graveyard. She saw a man of light who said, "Esther, come and follow me." What is your response to her dream? What role did it play in her story?

11. Soon after her unusual dream about the man of light, the author had unsettling conversations with two Christians, her classmate Azia and John at the medical lab. She said of John, "He wasn't cruel or full of hate; he was friendly and courteous." How did these conversations influence her opinion of Christians? What can we learn from these interactions?

12. After she became a Christian, the author began memorizing psalms. She writes, "There I found love, mercy, honest repentance, and the assurance of forgiveness. Islam had taught me to fear Allah, to never forget the prospect of eternal judgment and the brutal torture of hell. The psalms reminded me of the love of God—a love so great it overcomes all fear and death." What do you see as the main differences between the God of the Bible and the Qur'an's depiction of Allah?

13. In the Sermon on the Mount, Jesus spoke these words: "Blessed are those who are persecuted because of righteousness, for theirs is the kingdom of heaven. Blessed are you when people insult you, persecute you and falsely say all kinds of evil against you because of

me. Rejoice and be glad, because great is your reward in heaven, for in the same way they persecuted the prophets who were before you" (Matthew 5:10-12). How does Esther's experience of persecution relate to these verses? How do you react to Jesus' teaching on persecution?

14. In a debate with a cleric, Esther pointed out that the Qur'an confirms that Jesus performed miracles and raised people from the dead, but it does not record Muhammad performing any miracles. Esther's mother was healed of her heart condition. What role do you think this had in her coming to faith in Jesus Christ? Why do you think God might be using dreams and miracles among Muslims?

15. Esther says she learned about suffering from faithful Christians in Pakistan who were poor and marginalized, forced to rely on God alone. What do these stories of suffering Christians teach us about the value of suffering? Is suffering for being a Christian different from other types of suffering?

16. John and Esther were challenged to put their hope in God while they endured eight long years of waiting in Malaysia before they were able to go to the United States. Is there something you're waiting for now? What would it look like for you to trust God in your situation?

17. After Esther came to America, she observed that even though Christians can go to church without any restrictions, they often prefer to do other things instead. Do you think her observation is accurate? If so, why do you think that is true of some Christians in America?

18. When Esther, John, and Amiyah arrived in the States, they experienced life as refugees. She writes, "If you happen to meet a refugee or a family of refugees, don't rush away out of fear or uncertainty over what to say and do. Ask God how he is inviting you to be involved. . . . What would God have you do to reveal a little more of his love to them? . . . Ask them about their stories, and share your story too." Do you know any refugees? If so, what might you do to offer friendship to them? If not, how might you get connected with refugees in your area?

19. What new insights have you gained about growing up in a militant extremist community? In what ways does Esther's story inspire you in your own faith journey?

About the Authors

ESTHER AHMAD fled her home country of Pakistan due to life-threatening persecution for her Christian faith. She and her family were refugees in Malaysia for eight years; today, they reside in the American South. Esther shares her story of survival and redemption as she speaks to churches and organizations.

CRAIG BORLASE is a *New York Times* bestselling author who has written 50 books over the last two decades. He and his wife have four children and live in the English countryside.

Enjoy these other *great memoirs* from Tyndale Momentum.

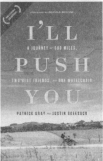

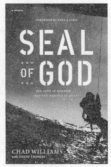